APQ LIBRARY OF
PHILOSOPHY

EDITED BY NICHOLAS RESCHER

RATIONAL BELIEF
SYSTEMS

BRIAN ELLIS

ROWMAN AND LITTLEFIELD
TOTOWA, NEW JERSEY

© *American Philosophical Quarterly 1979*

First published in the United States, 1979, by
Rowman and Littlefield, Totowa, New Jersey

Library of Congress Cataloging in Publication Data

Ellis, Brian David,1929–
  Rational belief systems.
  (APQ library of philosophy)
  Bibliography: p.
  1. Belief and doubt. 2. Logic. 3. Reasoning.
4. Rationalism. I. Title. II. Series.
BD215.E43   121'.6   78–11988
ISBN 0–8476–6108–3

Printed in Great Britain

10-12-84

TABLE OF CONTENTS

To Michael

INTRODUCTION

The laws of logic are the laws of thought. This is a doctrine which was popular in the last century, but is now very much out of favour. Nevertheless, I think it is true. The laws of logic are not, of course, universal generalizations about how ordinary people think. For, if they were they would all be false. But then, nor are the most basic laws of the physical sciences universal generalizations about how ordinary things behave in ordinary physical systems. For if they were, they would mostly be false too. Laws in science refer to idealized entities in idealized circumstances which model, usually less than perfectly, the real entities and circumstances of the physical world. They can be used to explain the behaviour of real entities, and the theories in which they are embedded provide frameworks for determining what remains to be explained. My thesis is that laws of logic are like this. They are laws governing the structure of ideally rational belief systems on idealized languages which model, always less than perfectly, ordinary human belief systems on natural languages. They can be used to explain at least some of the features of ordinary belief systems, and the theory of rational belief systems in which they are embedded provides a framework for determining what remains to be explained about our belief systems. It thus defines a research programme.

The theory of rational belief systems which is to be developed here is one which is consistent with a physicalist view of man. In fact, I suspect, it is the only coherent theory concerning our belief systems which is consistent with such a viewpoint. In many epistemologies it is assumed that man is a rational agent applying (or perhaps misapplying) certain *a priori* principles of reasoning to what is given to him through experience to construct his system of beliefs about reality.[1] The task of epistemology is seen as being to identify the given data, and the relevant principles of reasoning, and to show how those of our beliefs about the world which we are justified in holding might be constructed by reasoning according to these principles from what is given. If any of the principles required is not *a priori*, then the aim is to provide an *a priori* justification for its employment.[2] *The task of epistemology is seen as the rational reconstruction of knowledge.*

It is unnecessary to cite examples of such epistemologies, since it would be hard to find an empiricist epistemology (except, perhaps, Popper's) which did not take this view of the subject. Certainly, the epistemologies of the logical empiricists were reconstructivist; and even Popper, who rejects foundationalism and justificationism, sees the task of epistemology as a kind of rational reconstruction.[3] It is true that he regards his rational reconstruction as being only of the procedures for testing theories, and not of the thought processes which lead to them. But even so, he, like other epistemologists to whom he is opposed, thinks that there are certain *a priori* principles of reasoning (in his case, only the canons of deductive logic) which we, as rational agents, apply to the conjectures we have somehow made, or to the basic statements which we have decided to accept. This we do in the process of testing our theories, and building up the structure of objective science.

What all of these epistemologists share is a view of man as a more or less rational agent operating with *a priori* principles of reasoning upon given data (or in Popper's case upon conjectures and observationally acquired beliefs) to construct the edifice of objective scientific knowledge. All of them, including Popper,[4] think of the body of scientific knowledge as a kind of intellectual superstructure or building erected by us upon more or less firm foundations of items of knowledge or belief acquired directly through sense experience.

Yet is seems to me that this view of man is incompatible with the view which science requires us to take. For it is essentially a dualist one. It may not be dualist in the sense of presupposing the existence of two distinct kinds of substances, processes or events—mental and physical. But at least it implies that man, the rational agent, is somehow separate from the physical world which he is trying to understand. He is able to grasp certain *a priori* principles of reasoning which he can apply with varying degrees of facility to the items of belief or knowledge which he acquires through sense experience.

On the scientific view, man is a physical organism reacting in various ways to his environment. His beliefs are brain states of various kinds. His beliefs—all of them—are acquired by physical causal processes. Reasoning is such a process, and his reaching a conclusion a culmination of a physical process. A man's system of beliefs is a function of his genetic endowment and of the history of his sensory stimulation. His belief system would thus be better likened to an ecological system than to a building.[5] It has a certain shape and structure which can no doubt be explained. But the scientific explanation, when it is forthcoming, will not make reference to free agents applying or misapplying *a priori* rules of reasoning to given data. Rather I would expect it to proceed in two stages; firstly by the development of a theory of the structure and dynamics of human belief systems, and secondly by the development of a neurophysiological theory adequate to explain the relevant structural and dynamical laws. The view that human belief systems are products of human agency seems to me to be no more plausible than the view that ecological systems are products of divine agency.

My aim in this book is to begin the task of developing a *scientific epistemology*—one which is compatible with the austere physicalist view of man which I have just sketched. The theory of rational belief systems is concerned only with the first stage of the enquiry into how rational men think.[6] No one is yet in a position to say much about the underlying neurophysiological theory which will eventually be required. But I think we can say quite a lot about the structure and dynamics of rational belief systems.

It will be argued that the laws governing the structure and dynamics of rational belief systems are the laws of logic. That is, it will be argued that logic is properly founded in the theory of rationality.

Standardly, logical systems are founded on truth theories; so that truth is seen as being a more fundamental notion than that of rationality. On the standard account, if a system of beliefs can be said to be rational, it is only because these beliefs could all be true. Hence, if the account is not vacuous, knowledge of truth conditions should precede that of rationality. For some parts of natural languages, this view of the *epistemic* relationship between truth and rationality is plausible. For example, if "*F*" is a simple observational predicate of English, and "*a*" is a proper name, then we know that a rational belief system cannot include both the belief that *a* is *F* and also the belief that nothing is *F*. And, it is plausible to claim that this knowledge derives from our knowledge of the truth conditions for these two sentences (even if we should have some difficulty in articulating these conditions).

In general, however, the opposite seems to be the case. We can recognize a rational system of beliefs, or an irrational one, even where we cannot adequately specify truth conditions for the sentences in question. We do not even have to believe that the sentences involved are objectively true or false. Consequently, it is at least as plausible to maintain that knowledge of rationality precedes that of truth conditions. Therefore, a specification of rationality requirements on belief systems on a language may be at least as primitive, epistemically, as a truth theory for a language. Whether a truth theory for a language is adequate or not may thus come to be seen to depend on whether it yields the theory of rational belief systems for the language in question, rather than the converse.

It is commonly held that to understand a language sufficiently for logical purposes it is necessary to have a truth theory for it. But, if a theory of rational belief systems for a language is epistemically at least as primitive as a truth theory, then a truth theory may not be necessary. It may be sufficient if we have an adequate, recursive theory of rational belief systems for the language. If we have a truth theory as well, which yields the theory of rational belief systems, then so much the better. But it would be a mistake to insist that any adequate foundation for a logical system should proceed from an underlying truth theory.

An adequate truth theory for a language defines the language and determines the set of its tautologies. It does so by specifying (recursively, in a metalanguage) truth conditions for its sentences. An adequate theory of rational belief systems for a language also defines the language and determines the set of its tautologies. It does so by specifying (recursively, in a metalanguage) the conditions under which a truth or falsity claim concerning any sentence of the language may be incorporated into a rational system of beliefs on the language. More briefly, we may say that it does so by specifying acceptability conditions. The differences between truth and acceptability semantics thus reflect different analyses of understanding. On one analysis, to understand a sentence is to know what would make it true. On the other, it is to know what would make it acceptable. This essay assumes acceptability to be a more primitive notion than truth.

NOTES

1. Carnap's attempt in *Logical Foundations of Probability* and elsewhere to construct an *a priori* inductive logic is clearly part of this programme. Chisholm (1966) sees a need for some epistemic principles in addition to the canons of inductive and deductive logic. Popper (1934 and 1963a) rejects inductivism and

justificationism, but not constructivism. For him, the required method of reasoning is one of conjectures and refutations, and the basic data, by means of which refutations are effected are themselves low level conjectures which we, as agents, decide (for the time being at least) to accept.

2. The attempts of Reichenbach (1938) and Salmon (1961, 1963 and 1968) to vindicate induction are good examples of this. But see my (1965b) for the poverty of such vindications.

3. See Popper (1934), p. 31.

4. *Ibid.*, p. 111. "The empirical basis of objective science has nothing 'absolute' about it. Science does not rest upon rock bottom. The bold structure of its theories rises as it were, above a swamp. It is like a building erected upon piles. The piles are driven down from above into the swamp, but not down to any natural or 'given' base; and when we cease our attempts to drive our piles into a deeper layer, it is not because we have reached firm ground. We simply stop when we are satisfied that they are firm enough to carry the structure, at least for the time being."

5. This analogy is discussed and defended in Ellis (1975).

6. The theory of rational belief systems is sketched in Ellis (1976a). It is developed at greater length in a paper "The Dynamics of Belief Systems" which I read to the Australasian Association of Philosophy Conference in Melbourne in August 1976 and which is to appear in a Festschrift for D.A.T. Gasking edited by L. Chipman. It is further expanded and developed in this work.

Chapter I

The Ideal of Rationality

1. *Physical and Regulative Ideals*

Laws governing the behaviour of physical systems almost never apply directly to systems actually found in nature. They are nearly always stated for ideal types. The principles of particle dynamics, for example, are stated as laws governing the behaviour of idealized point masses in idealized systems called "inertial systems." The radiation laws apply only to perfectly black bodies, and the gas laws to perfect gases. The laws of conservation of energy and momentum apply only to closed and isolated systems. There are laws governing the behaviour of perfectly reversible heat engines, ideal, incompressible fluids, fluids in steady flow, chemical systems under constant conditions of temperature and pressure, and so on. There are idealizations in almost every branch of science, and the most fundamental laws of each field are usually formulated with reference to such idealizations. We should not, therefore, expect to be able to formulate any fundamental laws governing the structure and dynamics of human belief systems which will hold universally for all such systems. Rather, we should expect them to hold only for perfectly rational belief systems, i.e., the belief systems of ideally rational beings.

It is true that some philosophers would like to see a reconstruction of science which would remove all reference to such idealized entities, and allow the laws of nature to be expressed as universally quantified material conditionals. Quine and Smart,[1] for example, hold that an extensional language is (or should be) sufficient for all of the purposes of science. But whether such idealized entities are dispensable, even from ultimate science, is questionable. For Quine and Smart, ultimate science is purely descriptive of the world as it is. But I am inclined to think that ultimate science should be capable of explaining *why* things happen as they do, and that in order to do this, it must be capable of saying how things would have happened, if the world had been somehow different. I doubt whether Hempelian "covering law" explanations, which would appear to be the only kinds of explanations which could occur in Quine's or Smart's vision of ultimate science, would be satisfactory even there.

To know why something has happened is, at least in part, to know what contributions various factors have made to producing the effect. And to know this is to know what would have happened if this or that factor had not been present. To have understanding, therefore, we require knowledge of counterfactuals. We need to be able to formulate laws which tell us what would have happened in the absence of various disturbing factors—even if these factors are never in fact absent. Such laws will refer to idealized entities of various kinds. Therefore, if ultimate science is to be capable of explaining why things happen as they do, it must retain laws which refer to idealized entities. It must retain laws which can only be satisfactorily expressed as generalized counterfactual conditionals or nomic universals.

Quine or Smart might reply to this that we only feel the need for understanding (in my sense) *why* things happen because of the limitations of our knowledge. An omniscient being would have no need for such understanding, since he already knows what *will* happen. But since we have only a finite number of brain cells, we can hardly aspire to omniscience. We finite beings will have to lower our sights to a vision of ultimate science which is compatible with our finiteness. And such a science will retain idealized entities and nomic universals. For finite beings, ultimate science will contain simplifications and idealizations of infinitely complex nature.

But whatever view one takes of the desirability of aiming for an ultimate science in which all laws are expressed in a purely extensional language, I know of no way of achieving this objective. Therefore, I can see no good reason why extensionalist standards should be applied to any projected dynamics of belief systems. Therefore, it should not be a requirement on a theory of belief systems that its laws should hold for all ordinary human belief systems. What is required is only that the theory should provide a framework for *understanding* the structural and dynamical features of such belief systems.

Physical ideals provide a framework for understanding those physical systems which approximate to them. They enable us to say how the systems would behave if they were ideal. Deviations from ideal behaviour are then regarded as effects requiring independent causal explanation.[2] These become the targets for investigation. Perhaps the boundary conditions are not what we thought them to be. Perhaps there are other causal factors of which we have not taken account. When a system does not behave as we should expect it to, if it were ideal, it raises questions of this kind, and suggests lines of enquiry. The ideal thus generates a research programme. It is never enough just to say that the system does not behave ideally because it is not an ideal system (unless we are claiming that the system lies outside the intended scope of application of the theory). A more specific answer than this is required to explain the deviant behaviour. Ideally, we have to be able to say what the perturbing influences are, or how the boundary conditions differ from what we at first took them to be. And independent evidence for the satisfactoriness of these subsidiary explanations is required.[3]

Similarly, if the ideal of a rational man is to serve as a physical ideal, it should provide a framework for understanding the structure and behaviour of ordinary human belief systems. When someone appears to have a belief system which violates the requirements on ideally rational belief systems then the question is why? Perhaps he does not believe what we think he does, or even what *he* thinks he does. Perhaps he has some abnormal beliefs of which we have not yet taken account, but which, if taken account of, would alter our perception of the situation. Perhaps his belief system is in an unstable state, like an ecological system which has not yet fully adjusted to a new predator, so that the laws which we have formulated as governing the structure of stabilized rational belief systems do not apply. Perhaps his belief system is bifurcated into subsystems each of which can be successfully accommodated to the theory. No doubt there are other possibilities. But it should never be a sufficient explanation to say that the man is irrational, (any more than it is to say that a physical system is non-ideal), unless we mean thereby to say that his belief system is non-human or sub-human and so excluded from the intended scope of application of the theory.

The test of a theory of rational belief systems, like that of any other physical theory, is whether it generates a viable research programme. If it raises too many problems for explanation, which appear to be incapable of solution, then perhaps we should look again at our ideal of rationality. At this stage, our theory will have reached a crisis point, and a new theory will be required. Kuhn has described very well the kind of situation which can arise when a theory reaches breaking point.[4] But occasional difficulties, or a few recalcitrant phenomena, which have resisted explanation on the theory, do not constitute a crisis. By this last remark, I do not wish

to be taken as advocating unrestrained dogmatism or conventionalism. My target for criticism is naive falsificationism.[5] The
fact that a body falls when it is not supported is *prima facie*
evidence *against* Descartes' postulate that every body continues in
its state of rest or uniform motion in a straight line unless acted
upon by a force. Nevertheless, Newton was able to incorporate
Descartes' law into his comprehensive theory of gravitation; and
turn what was *prima facie* counterevidence to the law to his
advantage. The theory of rational belief systems is a physical
theory, and should be judged in the same way as other physical
theories.

The physical ideal of a rational belief system which I shall
propose is an ideal of rational equilibrium. It is like the concept of
a system of bodies in thermal equilibrium, or of a perfectly
balanced ecological system. Such states may never be realized in
any actual systems, but these concepts are useful all the same in
explaining the properties or structural features of actual systems.
An ideally rational belief system is one which is in equilibrium
under the most acute pressures of internal criticism and discussion.
Actual belief systems normally, and perhaps always, fail to be
ideally rational in this sense. This is so, partly because they are
continually being disturbed by new observationally (or otherwise)
acquired beliefs, and partly because the required pressures of
internal criticism and discussion are not applied, or if applied, not
understood, and so not effective. Nevertheless, as we shall see, the
physical ideal of a rational belief system is useful for explaining
some of the structural features of ordinary human belief systems.

Because the physical ideal of rationality is one of equilibrium, it
may also serve as a regulative ideal. For if we aspire to have a
belief system which is in equilibrium with respect to all pressures
of internal criticism and discussion, however well understood, then
we aspire to be rational according to this ideal of rationality. The
physical ideal would therefore serve as a regulative ideal to anyone
who wished to have a belief system of this kind. Whether one
should aspire to be rational according to this ideal, and if so why,
is a further question which will be taken up again in section 3 of
this chapter. But there is no doubt that most of us do wish to be
rational about what we believe to be the case, and that we share
certain basic intuitions about what it is to be rational. And the fact
that we have this desire and these intuitions supports the
hypothesis that being rational according to these intuitions has
some survival value. For, it would be difficult to explain their

existence, given the scientific view of man, on any other hypothesis. The kinds of intuitions which I have in mind about what a rational man may believe are almost universally shared, and therefore, presumably, not culturally determined.

It is possible that the regulative ideal of rationality which we undoubtedly possess is not the physical ideal required to explain the structural and dynamical features of human belief systems. But if so, then we have a further problem. For we should then have to explain why our regulative ideal is not effective in structuring our belief systems, and why, if it is not effective in this way, it should exist at all. What survival value could the ideal have if it were not a force in determining the shape of our belief systems? The simplest assumption to make is that the regulative ideal is the required physical ideal.

There are thus two requirements we should make on any ideal of rationality. Firstly, it should provide a framework for explaining the structural and dynamical features of human belief systems. That is, it should be a *physical* ideal. Secondly, it should be an ideal of rationality which accords with our most basic intuitions about what beliefs or combinations of beliefs a rational man may have, and hence about what kind of belief system we think an ordinary man ought to have. That is, it should be acceptable to the normal intellect as a *regulative* ideal.

2. *Rational Belief Systems*

A belief system is a set of beliefs. To describe a belief system we must say what beliefs occur in it. To do this we must at least say which sentences of a language are accepted as true, which are considered to be false, and which are not yet decided. Of course, such a description will be incomplete, because there are degrees of belief other than conviction of truth and falsity, and there may also be certain dynamical properties of belief systems which depend on how dogmatically beliefs are held. To begin with, however, it is enough to describe belief systems as sets of T, F and X evaluations over the sentences of some language, where $T\alpha$ is the firm belief that 'α' is true, $F\alpha$ the firm belief that 'α' is false, and $X\alpha$ occurs in a belief system B if 'α' would be evaluated in any other way (e.g., as probable or improbable) or not evaluated at all.

To describe an ideally rational belief system, it is likewise necessary to do so for some language. But to state the principles which govern structure of such belief systems, we should abstract from the grammatical and verbal particularities of natural languages, since we wish to develop theories which are applicable to belief systems generally, in whatever languages they may happen to be expressed. Accordingly, it is appropriate to state the principles governing the structure of ideally rational belief systems for various formal languages with vocabularies and syntactic structures which are designed to reflect the relevant features of natural languages. In this way we can achieve both greater simplicity and greater generality.

The standard approach to defining a belief system on a language is first to define a language by specifying truth conditions for its sentences, and then to define a belief system by specifying a set of T, F and X evaluations over its sentences. But I do not much like this approach for several reasons. Firstly, it restricts the range of languages which we may consider to those whose operators and connectives are truth functionally definable. Secondly, it limits consideration to languages, the sentences of which have specifiable truth conditions. Thirdly, it presupposes an untenable theory of meaning, viz., that the meaning of a sentence is determined by its truth conditions. Fourthly, it seems to require us to make sense of the idea that sentences (which are abstract third world entities) are the bearers of truth and falsity, and so presumably correspond or fail to correspond to reality. Fifthly, it assumes that languages can be defined independently of what anyone may believe. That is, it assumes that questions of meaning can be settled in advance of questions of truth. And finally, the traditional approach to defining a belief system, and ultimately a rational belief system on a language, is not in line with normal scientific practice.

I shall say more about these various points in chapter II. But first it is important to establish that a more direct approach to the study of rational belief systems is possible, and that in this way theories of rational belief systems can be developed in which the laws of the various standard logical systems can be derived.

The concept of an inertial system is not defined independently of the laws which govern the behaviour of Newtonian point masses in such systems. On the contrary, an inertial system is defined by Einstein as any system in which Newton's laws of motion hold good.[6] The concept of a Euclidean space is not defined independently of the laws governing the behaviour of Euclidean points, straight lines, triangles, etc., in such a space. On the contrary, the Euclidean axioms defining the behaviour of Euclidean points, straight lines, etc., serve to define a Euclidean space. Analogously, we should not expect the concept of a formal or ideal language to be defined independently of the laws which govern the structure of rational belief systems on that language. Rather, if these analogies are sound, we should define such languages as ones on which rational belief systems have the required structure.

The standard approach to the study of rational belief systems thus appears to be out of line with normal scientific practice. The approach which I advocate involves a direct attempt to discover some basic laws or axioms of rationality from which the various standard logical systems can be derived. These axioms, to be acceptable, should satisfy the two requirements on any ideal of rationality, and be formulated as laws governing the structure of ideally rational belief systems on appropriate formal languages. But the languages themselves need not be independently defined—except syntactically. For they will be sufficiently defined by the laws of rational belief systems upon them.

To illustrate this approach, consider the formal language L_0 with the syntactic structure of the sentential calculus. This is a language suitable for formulating some of the more fundamental laws governing the structure of rational belief systems. In general, to define the connectives and operators of a formal language L, and implicitly, a rational belief system on L, it is sufficient to state the relevant laws governing the structure of rational belief systems on L. In principle, this is like defining a Newtonian point mass, and implicitly an inertial system, by specifying the laws governing the behaviour of Newtonian point masses in inertial systems.

Let α and β be any two sentences of L_0. Then, by definition, a rational belief system B and L_0 satisfies the following conditions.

C1. One and only one of $T\alpha$, $F\alpha$ and $X\alpha$ occurs in B.

C2. α and $\sim\alpha$ do not occur with the same T or F evaluation in B.

C3. (a) $T(\alpha\vee\beta)$ occurs in B only if $F\alpha$ and $F\beta$ do not both occur in B.

    (b) $F(\alpha\vee\beta)$ occurs in B only if neither $T\alpha$ nor $T\beta$ occurs in B.

C4. (a) $T(\alpha\wedge\beta)$ occurs in B only if neither $F\alpha$ nor $F\beta$ occurs in B.

    (b) $F(\alpha\wedge\beta)$ occurs in B only if $T\alpha$ and $T\beta$ do not both occur in B.

C5. (a) $T(\alpha\supset\beta)$ occurs in B only if $T\alpha$ and $F\beta$ do not both occur in B.

       (b) $F(\alpha \supset \beta)$ occurs in B only if neither $F\alpha$ nor $T\beta$ occurs in B.

C6. (a) $T(\alpha \equiv \beta)$ occurs in B only if α and β do not occur with opposite T or F evaluations in B.

       (b) $F(\alpha \equiv \beta)$ occurs in B only if α and β do not occur with the same T or F evaluations in B.

C7. B is completable through every extension of L_0.

The concept of completability occurring in C7 will be explained in the following section. But first some general remarks. The laws C1 to C6 are very weak indeed, and I am grateful to Dr. Richards for pointing out to me just how weak it is possible to make them. They are so weak that without the condition C7 it cannot even be demonstrated that $T(p \wedge \sim p)$ does not occur in any rational belief system on L_0. The law C1 is a general law governing the structure of any rational belief system, and I do not imagine that it is likely to be dropped from any future theory of rational belief systems. The laws C2 to C6 are as much linguistic competence requirements as rationality laws, since they serve to define the connectives and operators of L_0. If a belief system on a language syntactically like L_0 violated any of these laws, then either it is not rational, or it is not a belief system on L_0. The law C7, like C1, is a general principle of rationality. It is more controversial than C1, but it satisfies the requirements on an ideal of rationality.

By an extension of a language, I mean any language with the given syntactic structure which includes the given language. By a completion of a belief system B on a language L, I mean any belief system on L which includes all of the T and F evaluations which occur in B, and no X evaluations, and is rational according to the remaining criteria. Thus, if B is a belief system on L_0, then B is completable on L_0 if it is possible to replace every X evaluation which occurs in B with a T or F evaluation without violating any of the laws C1 to C6. And B is a rational belief system on L_0 only if B is completable through every extension of L_0.

The laws C1 to C7 provide a sufficient basis for the sentential calculus. For it is not difficult to prove that α is a theorem of the sentential calculus if $F\alpha$ does not occur in any rational belief system on L_0. I define a tautology of a language as any sentence of the language which a rational man cannot deny. It follows that the tautologies of L_0 are just the valid wffs of SC.

This simple example illustrates what I mean by defining languages by specifying laws governing the structure of rational belief systems upon them. The language L_0 and the logical connectives and operators of L_0 are defined in this way at least as well as inertial systems and mass points are defined in Newtonian mechanics. Whether the language provides a satisfactory model for analysing the structure of belief systems expressed in natural languages is a further question. It is like the question of whether Newtonian mechanics provides a satisfactory framework for analysing the motions of physical particles, and should be decided in the same kind of way.

3. The Ideal of Completability

The principle of completability, which requires that a rational belief system be completable through every extension of the language, is an ideal of rationality which nearly everyone shares. For it is implied by the requirement that a rational belief system be defensible against all internal criticism. By internal criticism, I mean any which depends solely upon argument by *reductio ad absurdum*. A belief system B which failed to satisfy this principle could always be refuted to the satisfaction of a rational, competent speaker of the language by such an argument, provided that the language in question did not contain any sentences which could not become accepted as true or false. For, it would always be sufficient to point out to him that, however he might decide on what he remained undecided about, he would be in violation of some other rationality requirement. A belief system B is rational, therefore, only if it is completable in the sense that there is some way of replacing the X evaluations which occur in B by T or F evaluations. In natural languages, new terms and predicates are constantly being added as new objects and properties are discovered. Therefore, a rational belief system on a natural language, and hence on any idealized model of a natural language, should not only be completable on the language as it presently stands, but through all extensions of that language.

I do not know of any satisfactory way of justifying the ideal of completability, and in the final analysis, I do not think that any justification is possible. One could, if one wished, introduce a truth predicate and a quotation operator into one's language, and make the requirement that "True 'α' " and 'α' do not occur with opposite T or F evaluations in any rational belief system B on the language. Then "True 'α' $\equiv \alpha$" would be a tautology of the enriched language. And it could then be said that a belief system B is rational only if the truth of everything that is thought to be known, i.e., receives a

T evaluation in *B*, could be maintained against all internal criticism. But a truth predicate, introduced in this way, while it satisfies Tarski's convention *T*, is a purely formal predicate which does nothing but enable us to restate the principle of completability in another way.

By a purely formal predicate, I mean one which can be defined formally and adequately simply by specifying rationality requirements on belief systems on languages which contain it—and defined without reference to any other predicates of any of these languages. Another predicate of this kind is "materially implies". The reformulation of the principle of completability using the truth predicate would be more interesting if "true" signified a substantive and objective property, rather than a purely formal one. The predicate "has a rest mass of less than 10 grams" signifies something approximating to a substantive and objective property. It is substantive in the sense that it cannot be defined purely formally, and it is objective in the sense that competent speakers of the language who understand the surrounding theory can reach mutual and independent accord on the applicability of this predicate. And where, in borderline cases, they may disagree, they will normally, after consultation and review of evidence, be able to resolve their differences. This leads us to the view that there is a correct or true answer to the question of whether a given object satisfies this predicate, since this common experience causes us to accept the generalization that such accord on the applicability of this predicate is always possible.

Having made this inference, we believe that it cannot be just a coincidence that we can reach independent accord. There must be some causal factors in the world which operate to produce it. And, by Mill's method of difference, we reason that those causal factors must be present in the objects themselves. Thus, we are led to the view that the predicate "has a rest mass of less than 10 grams" uniquely and objectively divides the objects in the universe into two mutually exclusive and jointly exhaustive classes—those which satisfy it, and those which do not. Those which satisfy it are those which have within them the power to produce in us in the appropriate circumstances the belief that they have a rest mass of less than 10 grams. A predicate like this I call an objective predicate. In this case, it corresponds to a power or property in the objects which satisfy it.

If all of the predicates of our language were like this, and all sentences truth functional, then truth as formally defined would also be an objective and substantive predicate. For it would divide the beliefs which we could have on the language into two mutually exclusive and jointly exhaustive classes in an objective fashion. Tarski's theory of truth, in that it relies upon a primitive notion of satisfaction of predicates by objects is thus a kind of correspondence theory of truth, and it seems to me that such a theory is entirely appropriate for those fragments of natural languages in which all of the substantive predicates are objective and all of the connectives and operators truth functional.

However, many predicates of natural languages are not objective in this sense, and there is lacking a basis of independent accord for the inference to corresponding properties in nature. Moreover, many connectives, such as the subjunctive "if ... then ...", and the various modal operators, are not truth functional, and for languages which include such predicates, operators and connectives, a correspondence theory is neither required nor appropriate. But this does not mean that we cannot define rational belief systems on such languages. Obviously, we must be able to if there are valid arguments involving such predicates, connectives and operators. The mistake is to suppose that for a belief system on a language to be rational it must be possible for every belief included in it to be true in any other than a purely formal sense.

As a justification for being rational, the claim that only if one is rational could all of one's beliefs be true, is in any case a weak justification. For why be so cautious? If we applied this principle to betting on horses then we should never take more than one bet on any one race, on the grounds that if we did so, then not all of our bets could win. What is so important about having a system of beliefs all of which could be true? And if it is important, how does being rational help us to achieve this objective? At best, it is only a condition of the possibility of achieving it. Hence the usual justification for being rational is not sufficient. What would have to be shown in detail is how being fully rational according to certain ideals of rationality would better serve some human interest, such as our survival, then any alternative, and would do so even if not all of our beliefs were true or false in any substantive or objective sense.

The question "Why be rational?" should be transformed into the question "Why do human beings have certain ideals of rationality, and how does our having such ideals serve our interests?" This question presumably has an answer. It is like the question "Why do human beings feel pain?" I do not believe that it is just an accidental by-product of human evolution that we have these ideals, or that our having them has been culturally determined. Our rationality has almost certainly been a major factor in our survival as a species. Therefore, it is probable that our having these ideals of rationality is genetically determined. But I do not yet know how our ideals of rationality contribute to our survival as a species. And I doubt whether anyone will be able to say so, until we know a great deal more about the dynamics of belief systems, and the causal rôles they have in determining human choices and actions.

4. *P-Completability*

We have so far described a belief system as a set T, F and X evaluations over the sentence of a language. But such a description takes no account of the fact that beliefs can be held with various degrees of confidence. We have said that $T\alpha$ occurs in one's belief system B iff one is convinced that α, that $F\alpha$ occurs in B iff one is convinced that it is not the case that α, and that in any other case, $X\alpha$ occurs in B. But there is clearly a difference between being fairly sure that α and fairly sure that not α, and these two states of belief cannot co-exist in a rational belief system. Therefore, neither state of belief is adequately described by saying that $X\alpha$ occurs in B. Yet in the metalanguage we have so far used this is all we could say.

Let us enrich the metalanguage by introducing a scale of degrees of belief, the measures on which will be subjective probabilities or P-evaluations. A belief system may then be described as a set of such evaluations over the sentences of some language. However, to allow for the possibility of some indeterminacy in our degrees of belief, let us say that if an individual has no determinate degree of belief concerning a sentence α of the language, or can only fix it to within a certain range, then $Y\alpha$ occurs in his belief system. Accordingly, a belief system B on a language L will now be described as a set of P or Y evaluations over the sentences of L. The term "$P\alpha$" will be used to signify the P evaluation of α. T and F evaluations are now to be regarded as the extreme P evaluations. For the time being however, we shall continue to use T and F evaluations, as well as P and Y evaluations in our descriptions of belief systems.

Let B be a belief system on a language L. Then we have argued that B is rational only if B is completable through every extension of L. This requirement may now be supplemented by the requirement of P-completability. A P-completion of a belief system B is a belief system obtained from B simply by replacing all Y evaluations by P evaluations without violating any of the other requirements on such evaluations. A belief system B on a language L is P-completable iff there is a P completion of B through every extension of L.

The requirement of P-completability, like that of completability, derives from the general concept of a rational belief system as one which is in equilibrium under all pressures of internal criticism and discussion. If a belief system B were not P-completable, then it could always be refuted by a *reductio ad absurdum* argument, once the P-evaluations in B were explicitly acknowledged. For it would be sufficient to point out that however the remaining Y evaluations might be replaced by P-evaluations some violation of the other requirements on P evaluations would occur.

Let B_0 be any P-completable belief system on a language L, and B any P-completion of B_0. For B to exist, B_0 must be completable. My requirements on B are:

A1.   (a) $P_{max}\alpha$ occurs in B, if $F\alpha$ does not occur in any completed extension of B_0

        (b) $P_{min}\alpha$ occurs in B, if $T\alpha$ does not occur in any completed extension of B_0.

A2. $P\alpha = P\beta$ in B if $P_{max}(\alpha \equiv \beta)$ occurs in B.

A3. $P(\alpha \vee \beta) \geq P\alpha$ in B; and if $P_{min}\beta$ occurs in B, then $P(\alpha \vee \beta) = P\alpha$.

A4. $P(\alpha \vee \beta)$ is a strictly monotonic increasing function of $P\alpha$ and $P\beta$ if $P_{min}(\alpha \wedge \beta)$ occurs in B.

These four requirements ensure that the logical operation of disjoining any two sentences α and β of L is formally an addition operation if $P_{min}(\alpha \wedge \beta)$ occurs in B. Therefore, in order to define a scale of subjective probability we may set $P(\alpha \vee \beta) = P\alpha + P\beta$ in cases where $P_{min}(\alpha \wedge \beta)$ occurs in B. Conventionally, the maximum and minimum values on the scale are set equal to 1 and 0 respectively.

Given these scaling conventions, it is easy to prove that in any P-completed belief system B

P1. $0 \leq P\alpha \leq 1$

P2. $P(\alpha \vee \sim\alpha) = 1$

P3. $P\alpha + P\sim\alpha = 1$

P4. $P(\alpha \vee \beta) = P\alpha + P\beta - P(\alpha \wedge \beta)$

and hence that the P evaluations occurring in B are, formally, probability measures. The derivations of P1 to P3 are obvious. To derive P4, we have by A3 that

$$P(\alpha \vee \beta) := P(\alpha \vee (\sim\alpha \wedge \beta))$$
$$= P\alpha + P(\sim\alpha \wedge \beta)$$

and that

$$P\beta = P((\alpha \wedge \beta) \vee (\sim\alpha \wedge \beta))$$
$$= P(\alpha \wedge \beta) + P(\sim\alpha \wedge \beta)$$

Hence

$$P(\alpha \vee \beta) = P\alpha + P\beta - P(\alpha \wedge \beta).$$

The requirements A1 to A4 are rationality requirements of the kind I am seeking. Of these, only A4 is likely to be at all controversial. What it says, in effect, is that if anyone is convinced that 'α' and 'β' cannot both be true then his degree of belief in the disjunction of α and β should depend *only* upon his degrees of belief in the disjuncts, and the more probable he thinks them to be, the more probable he should think their disjunction to be. It is a consequence of A4 that if $P\alpha = P\gamma$ and $P\beta = P\delta$ in B, and $P_{min}(\alpha \wedge \beta)$ and $P_{min}(\gamma \wedge \delta)$ both occur in B, then $P(\alpha \vee \beta) = P(\gamma \vee \delta)$ in B.

Note that the requirements A1 to A4 are all *comparative*, and do not depend for their acceptability upon the adoption of any particular *scale* for the measurement of degrees of belief. The requirements only show that a particular kind of scale (viz., a 0 to 1 additive scale) is particularly appropriate for measuring degrees of belief, and that if such a scale is adopted, then the measures on this scale will be probability measures in the formal sense of the probability calculus.

Scales of measurement are adopted for various historical and practical reasons, and I have no doubt that the scale of measurement we use for subjective probability derives from the historical connection between probability theory and gambling. If it were not for this connection a -1 to $+1$ scale might well have been used. It is no accident, however, that an additive scale for subjective probability has been adopted. For the operation of disjoining mutually exclusive alternatives is formally an addition operation with respect to degree of belief. It is usually a mistake to try to define a quantity, or even a scale for the measurement of a quantity, operationally.[7] For most of our quantity and scale concepts are cluster concepts. Degree of belief is no exception. A person's degree of belief in a proposition is not to be identified with what he would consider to be a fair betting quotient for that proposition, since taking his assessment for a fair betting quotient for that proposition is just one means among several we have of measuring his degree of belief in it. Moreover, it is demonstrable that this procedure will only yield a measure of his degree of belief if he has no doubt that the bet will be decided.[8]

Degree of belief is in fact also measurable *fundamentally* by procedures which depend only upon our being able to make comparative probability judgements, since for natural languages the postulate A5 is satisfied.

A5.   For any sentence γ of L such that $P_{\min}\gamma$ does not occur in B, there exists a set α_1, α_2, ... α_n of mutually exclusive, jointly exhaustive and subjectively equiprobable sentences of L such that $P\alpha_i < P\gamma$, and there is a number $k \leq n$ such that $P(\alpha_1 \vee \alpha_2 ... \alpha_k) \geq P\gamma$ in B.

The conditions A1 to A5 together ensure that subjective degree of belief is a *fundamentally measurable quantity* like length or mass or time-interval. There is no need, therefore, to rely upon subjective determinations of fair betting quotients to measure degrees of belief. We need no more than criteria for determining equality or inequality of degree of belief to determine a measure of degree of belief on a probability scale.

The measures of degrees of belief which we can make by any of these procedures are no doubt fairly crude by most standards in the physical sciences. Nevertheless, P-evaluations are normally determinable to within a fairly narrow range. Indeed, a range of some kind if always determinable—even if it is only 0 to 1. A belief system B on a language L may therefore be described as a set of P or of *ranges of P* evaluations over the sentences of L. Given this way of describing belief systems, the requirement of P-completability should be that the P evaluations can be made *within the specified ranges* compatibly with the other P evaluations and the requirements A1 to A4. Given this stronger P completability principle, and adopting the usual scale for measuring degrees of belief, the two requirements of completability and P-completability may now be combined into a single principle: *A belief system B on a language L is rational only if any indeterminate or vaguely* specified degrees of belief occurring in *B* can be specified precisely within these limits of vagueness so that the resulting system of *P* evaluations over the sentences of *L* satisfy the axioms of the probability calculus—and this process can be carried out through every extension of *L*. For it is demonstrable that such a belief system *B* is *P* completable only if it is completable.

5. The Logical Correspondence Principle

If *T* and *F* evaluations over the sentences of a language can be identified as subjective probability evaluations of 1 and 0, then it follows that the logic of truth and falsity claims is a logic of certainty, i.e., a logic derivable from a two valued probability calculus in which the range of possible probability values is restricted to 1 and 0. There should thus be a kind of correspondence between two-valued logical systems and probability theories. In particular, if α is a tautology of a two valued logical system, then $P(\alpha) = 1$ should be a theorem of some corresponding probability theory, and conversely. I call the requirement that such a correspondence should exist *the logical correspondence principle*.

The classical probability calculus, PRC, has an absolute fragment, PRC_0, which contains all and only those theorems which do not involve conditional probabilities. It is well known that this fragment has a subjectivist logical interpretation, and that on this interpretation $P(\alpha) = 1$ is a theorem of PRC_0 iff α is a valid wff of the sentential calculus, SC. PRC_0 thus interpreted and SC therefore satisfy the logical correspondence principle. It can be shown, however, that PRC_0 does not provide an adequate sentential logic of subjective probability. To analyse arguments involving subjective probability claims on conditional sentences (not only on subjunctive conditionals, but also ordinary indicative conditionals) we appear to need the full apparatus of PRC. Subjective probability claims on conditionals appear to behave as conditional probability claims on their consequents given their antecedents.[10] This would not matter if PRC and SC also satisfied the logical correspondence principle. But demonstrably they do not do so. For $P((\beta \lor \sim\beta)/(\alpha \lor \sim\alpha)) = 1$ is a theorem of PRC, but $(\beta \lor \sim\beta)/(\alpha \lor \sim\alpha)$ is not a *wff*, and so not a valid *wff* of SC.

I would have no objection to PRC_0 as a basic logic of subjective probability or to SC as a basic logic of truth and falsity claims, if neither was intended to be used to analyse arguments involving truth, falsity or probability claims on conditionals. For then, both would be adequate for their limited purposes, but admittedly inadequate as sentential logics.

But when the attempt is made to construe conditionals as material conditionals, whether within the context of truth or falsity claims or within that of probability claims the results are grossly counterintuitive. The paradoxes of material implication are well known. But the probabilistic paradoxes of material implication although less well-known are far more serious. With the ordinary paradoxes, at least it can be argued, with some plausibility, that they result from a failure to distinguish clearly between truth and assertability conditions. Moreover, it can be argued that if a conditional is not a material conditional, then it is not truth functionally definable; and if it is not truth functionally definable, then a satisfactory Tarskian truth theory for a language in which it occurs (which is compatible with empiricism, and which explains how the language is learnable) cannot be given. Hence, it may be argued that if the conditionals of ordinary language are not material conditionals, then so much the worse for ordinary language.[11] But neither of these replies can deal with the probabilistic paradoxes. Despite Lewis' arguments to the contrary,[12] there are no confusions of assertability with truth conditions which would account for the counterintuitive results, and there is already available a probability calculus, PRC, which is as well founded as its absolute fragment, PRC_0, and which in all ordinary cases, can be used satisfactorily to analyse arguments involving subjective probability claims on conditionals.

The most important probabilistic paradoxes derive from the theorem T1 of PRC_0:

T1. $P(\alpha \supset \beta) + P(\sim\alpha \supset \beta) \geq 1$.

From this theorem it follows that

(1) $P(\alpha \supset \beta) < \frac{1}{2}$, and
(2) $P(\sim\alpha \supset \beta) < \frac{1}{2}$

cannot both occur in any rational belief system on the language. Hence, if the indicative conditionals of English are material conditionals, then the following two statements:

(3) If the Liberals are re-elected, then Mr. Whitlam will be appointed Governor General, and

(4) If the Liberals are not re-elected, then Mr. Whitlam will be appointed Governor General

cannot both be judged to be improbable, i.e., if one has a low degree of belief in one of them, then one should have a high degree of belief in the other. But it is absurd to argue from the improbability of (3) to the probability of (4). Hence the paradox.

I do not see any satisfactory way of arguing that this paradox results from any confusions of truth with assertability conditions. To do so, it would appear to be necessary to argue that a subjective probability claim on a conditional does not express a degree of belief in its *truth*, but rather expresses its degree of *assertability*. Lewis has in fact argued precisely this.[13] However, for reasons to be explained later, I remain to be convinced by his arguments.

It might be suggested that the improbability claims concerning (3) and (4) should properly be represented by the mixed SC and PRC_0 formulae:

(5) $\alpha \supset (P(\beta) < \frac{1}{2})$,

and

(6) $\sim\alpha \supset (P(\beta) < \frac{1}{2})$.

But this suggestion gives rise to other difficulties, since the following argument is obviously invalid:

It is improbable that Mary will go if I do
It is probable that Mary will go if John does

∴ Either John or I will not go,

while the corresponding formal argument:

$\alpha \supset (P(\beta) < \frac{1}{2})$
$\gamma \supset (P(\beta) > \frac{1}{2})$

∴ $\sim\alpha \vee \sim\gamma$

is valid.

There is, however, normally no need even to try to construe conditionals within probability contexts as material conditionals when assessing the validity of arguments involving them. For the two improbability claims concerning (3) and (4) can be represented without difficulty or paradox as the conditional probability claims:

(7) $P(\beta/\alpha) < \frac{1}{2}$
(8) $P(\beta/\sim\alpha) < \frac{1}{2}$

The formulae, (7) and (8), are consistent, and together they imply (as they should) $P(\beta)<\frac{1}{2}$. Moreover, from $P(\beta/\alpha)<\frac{1}{2}$ and $P(\beta/\gamma)>\frac{1}{2}$ no paradoxical consequences follow. Conditional probability claims are, therefore, demonstrably better representations of probability claims concerning conditionals than probability claims concerning material conditionals. If one has a better theory, already available, why bother to try to patch up a theory which is clearly in deep trouble.

Let us accept, then, that within the context of a probability claim, a conditional, whether it be a subjunctive or an indicative, is not a material conditional, and that a probability claim on a conditional behaves much more like a conditional probability claim. Then, applying the logical correspondence principle, we may conclude that, even within the context of a truth or falsity claim, a conditional is not a material conditional. Hence, SC cannot be an adequate sentential logic for a language in which conditionals occur. What the required sentential logic may be, we cannot yet say. But we may be sure that it is derivable as a logic of certainty from a satisfactory logic of subjective probability, and that such a logic will look very like the classical probability calculus PRC.

It is easy to prove that $P(\beta/\alpha)=1$ entails $P(\alpha\supset\beta)=1$, and that $\{P(\alpha)\neq 0,\ P(\alpha\supset\beta)=1\}$ entails $P(\beta/\alpha)=1$. Therefore, if PRC is accepted as providing a satisfactory sentential logic of subjective probability claims, then, in the corresponding logic of truth claims, there must be a conditional, '$\rightarrow$', which has at least the following properties:

(1) $T(\alpha\rightarrow\beta)$ occurs in a rational belief system B only if $F(\alpha\supset\beta)$ does not occur in B
(2) $F(\alpha\rightarrow\beta)$ occurs in B only if $T(\alpha\supset\beta)$ does not occur in B or $F\alpha$ occurs in B.

From these requirements, and that of completability it is easy to prove that

(3) $(\alpha\rightarrow\beta)\supset(\alpha\supset\beta)$ and
(4) $(\alpha\wedge\beta)\supset(\alpha\rightarrow\beta)$

must be tautologies of the language in which B is expressed.

There are reasons, however, for thinking that PRC is not an adequate logic of subjective probability. Firstly, in the classical calculus, $P(\beta/\alpha)$ is undefined, if $P\alpha=0$. This restriction would have to be overcome—perhaps in the way that Popper has suggested.[14] Secondly, compound conditionals (i.e., sentences in which conditionals occur within the scopes of other logical connectives or operators) are undefined in classical probability theory. This restriction would also have to be overcome, and in a way which was not open to Lewis' objections.[15] This problem will be taken up and discussed in Chapter III.

NOTES

1. See Quine (1954) and Smart (1968), p. 164.

2. I have discussed this concept of an effect in my (1963), (1965a) and (1976b). In these works, the discussion is concerned mainly with dynamical effects. But what I have to say there has wider application. In general, physical laws determine ideals of behaviour. They do not describe the actual behaviour of ordinary physical systems. They say only how these systems would behave if they were ideal. Similarly, we should not expect the laws of rationality to describe the actual thought behaviour of ordinary human beings. Rather, we should expect such laws to describe the thought behaviour of ideally rational beings, and to provide only a framework for explaining how ordinary human beings think. Given such a framework, the effects to be explained are deviations from the rational ideal.

3. The kind of process I have in mind is well described in Lakatos (1970) p. 118, where he speaks of "theoretically progressive problem shifts".

4. See Kuhn (1962).

5. See Lakatos (1970), pp. 116 ff.

6. Einstein (1905) pp. 37–8.

7. For a defence of this position see Ellis (1966) chs. 2 and 3.

8. This is demonstrated in Ellis (1973) section 3.

9. This logical correspondence principle is discussed also in Ellis (1973) section 1.

10. This fact has been noted by several other authors, including Adams (1965) and (1966), Stalnaker (1968) and Lewis (1976b).

11. Smart (1968) takes this line.

12. In his (1976b).

13. See Lewis (1976b) for details.

14. See Popper (1955).

15. I am referring to the triviality results proved in Lewis (1976b).

Chapter II

The Laws of Rationality

The central thesis of this chapter is that the laws of logic are laws governing the structure of rational belief systems. To establish this thesis, I will show how the theorems of the various standard logical systems can all be demonstrated to be tautologies of appropriate formal languages, if certain basic requirements are made on the structure of rational belief systems on those languages. The basic requirements I have in mind are either general rationality requirements, like the requirement of completability discussed in Chapter I (which must be satisfied by a rational belief system on any language) or specific requirements on the structure of rational belief systems on particular formal languages which are otherwise defined only syntactically. The specific rationality requirements will implicitly define the logical connectives and operators of these languages and hence the languages themselves. Formally, my procedure here will be like the standard scientific procedure in defining Newtonian mass-points and inertial systems by specifying the laws governing the behaviour of mass-points in such systems.[1]

1. *Critique of Classical Semantics*

Standardly, *a language* is defined by specifying truth conditions recursively for its sentences, and a belief system on a language, so defined, is said to be *rational* iff all of the sentences of the language believed to be true or believed to be false could indeed be true or false, respectively. I shall postpone discussion of this concept of rationality until later. Here I wish to concentrate on the standard or classical approach to defining a language.

My first objection is that this approach limits the range of languages we may consider to those in which the connectives and operators are truth functionally definable. If the actual world is the only world, as Quine believes, then the modal operators are not truth functionally definable. Therefore, languages which include the modal operators cannot be classically defined. Therefore, the rationality of a belief system on a modal language cannot in general be determined. Therefore, we should cease to use such languages, and say what we wish to say in a non-modal language.

Discourse in a modal language is second grade discourse.[2] If, however, the actual world is not the only world, as Lewis believes,[3] and certain kinds of relationships connect them, then the modalities are truth functionally definable, and a rational belief system on a modal language is also definable. But then, since possible worlds cannot interact, I cannot see what human interest could be served by having a rational belief system on such a language. *What does it matter what we believe obtains in worlds other than our own?* It cannot possibly make any difference to us whether what we believe about them is true or false.

My second objection is that if adequate truth conditions for the sentences of a language cannot be specified, then the language is ill-defined, and so is the concept of a rational belief system on the language. The requirement that a language be defined adequately for the purposes of logic thus gives rise to a programme of logical analysis. Logical analysts assume that there is a certain class of sentences of any language for which " 'α' is true iff α" is a sufficient analysis. Such sentences are usually called "basic sentences" or "protocol sentences", and they are variously identified according to which doctrine of "the given" is accepted. Any sentence which does not belong to the basic class requires further logical analysis, and the attempt to provide such analyses has been a preoccupation of philosophers of science since the days of the Vienna Circle. But the programme has met with singularly little success,[4] and many philosophers of science have now abandoned the attempt to discover such analyses, even for the concepts of empirical science. The concepts of evidential support, causality, probability, and nomic necessity have all defied attempts to find adequate empiricist analyses.[5] It is time to question whether the whole idea of trying to define a language by specifying truth conditions for its sentences is not misguided.

Thirdly, the classical approach derives from an analysis of meaning or understanding which is untenable, viz., that to understand a sentence is to know its truth conditions. For if this were correct, then "$2+2=4$" and "There is no decision procedure for the predicate calculus" would be understood to mean the same; since both are true in all possible worlds. Logical empiricists used to reply to this by making a distinction between meaning and empirical significance. The quoted sentences have the same empirical significance, but not the same meaning. The distinction relegates talk about meaning to second grade discourse and restricts attention to empirical significance.[6] But the question of what a sentence means is far too important to be so put aside. From a logical empiricist's point of view, the theorems of logic and mathematics are all just so many different ways of saying the same thing, viz., nothing.

My fourth objection to defining a language by specifying truth conditions for its sentences is that it appears to make sentences the bearers of truth and falsity. But from a physicalist point of view, it is hard to see how such an abstract third world (i.e., neither mental nor physical) entity as a sentence could bear the required relationship of correspondence to reality. An utterance might conceivably do so, since it is a physical event which might perhaps bear some kind of physical correspondence relationship to the events of which it speaks. And a belief might do so, since it is presumably a physical state of the brain, and such a state certainly bears some kind of relationship to the causes of its production. But I have no satisfactory model for a truth relationship between such abstract entities as sentences and physical reality.

A sentence might be a sentence of more than one language. Therefore the same sentence might be both true in one language and false in another. So sentences as such cannot be the bearers of truth. Only a sentence of a given language could be a bearer of truth. But if the language contains tensed verbs, token reflexives, demonstratives or ambiguous terms, as all natural languages do, then a sentence might be true in one context and false in another or true when understood in one way, and false when understood in another. So only a sentence of a given language in a given context, as uttered by a given person and understood in a given way (or alternatively, only a sentence of a very special kind of language), could be a bearer of truth. But once the doctrine that sentences are the bearers of truth has been so qualified, we are left with the uneasy feeling that sentences are not the bearers of truth after all. It is as though I were to hold that *the phrase* "The first professor of philosophy at La Trobe" is married to Jenny Ellis, and then, as objections are raised, qualify this to the claim that this phrase, uttered now, and understood as referring to me, is married to Jenny Ellis. Certainly, a relationship of some kind will hold between that phrase so monstrously qualified and Jenny Ellis iff I am married to Jenny Ellis. But the relationship between the phrase and my wife is not that of marriage.[7] Similarly, while there might be some kind of correspondence relationship which holds between a sentence of a given language in a given context as uttered by a given person and understood in a given way, and reality, I see no reason to suppose that this correspondence relationship is that of truth.

The same kind of thing happens when one considers utterances to be the bearers of truth and falsity. Since utterances of sentences do not tell us to which languages they belong, the same utterance might be both true and false. I might, for example, be bilingual and intend by means of the one utterance to say one thing to one half of my audience, and another thing to the other half. But one of these things might be true, and the other false. Therefore, if utterances, as such, were the bearers of truth and falsity, the one utterance could be both. So at best, utterances of sentences of a given language are the bearers of truth and falsity. But natural languages contain ambiguous terms. I might, for example, say to Fred and Mary that Susan passed her exam, knowing that Fred knows one and only one person called Susan, and that Mary also knows one and only one such person, and that the person Fred knows is not the person Mary knows. Moreover, I might utter this sentence intending to say to each that *their* Susan passed her exam. But these statements might have different truth values. Therefore, at best, utterances of sentences of a given language understood in a given way are the bearers of truth and falsity.

The most plausible remaining candidates for the rôle of bearers of truth and falsity are beliefs. I do not wish to defend this claim here, or to consider such other candidates as thoughts or propositions, since my aim is only to present a critique of the classical approach to defining a language by specifying truth conditions for its sentences. Here my focus has been upon the apparent implication of this approach that sentences are the bearers of truth and falsity. I have argued that for natural languages this thesis is untenable, and I would conclude that even for a formal language, in which there might be assumed to exist a one-one correlation between sentences and belief states, it must be rejected. The quoted sentences in the *T*-sentences of a truth theory, which is proposed to define a formal language, should be understood as referring to the corresponding beliefs. Thus

$\quad$ 'α' is true iff β

should be read as

$\quad$ The belief expressed by 'α' is true iff β.

My fifth objection is that the classical approach assumes that languages can be defined independently of what anyone may believe. On the contrary, I would suppose that how a person understands the logical connectives and operators of a language, and hence what language he speaks, depends upon the broad pattern of acceptances and rejections which his belief system displays. To suppose that someone could understand the connectives and operators as we do, and yet *systematically* violate requirements like C1 to C4 is like supposing that there could be an elephant which had the anatomy and physiology of a horse. I am willing to allow that there may be unusual or deviant elephants, and I concede that there may be deviant belief systems on languages like L_0 in which occasional violations of, say, C1 to C4 occur. But a horse is not an elephant, and a belief system in which any of C1 to C4 is *systematically* violated is not a belief system on a language of this kind.

To define the connectives and operators of a formal language, it is perhaps contingently sufficient to specify a truth theory for that language. But then the connectives and operators of the formal language can be no better understood than those of that fragment of the natural language in which the truth theory is (ultimately) specified. A person who accepts a given truth theory for a formal language, in the sense that he assents to the various *T*-sentences which comprise the truth theory, may be presumed to understand the connectives and operators of the *formal* language in the same way as other speakers of his language. But this is so only because he can be presumed to understand the connectives and operators of his natural language in the same way as others. And if there are any doubts about this, then these same doubts must flow through to become doubts about how he understands the connectives and operators of the formal language. The connectives and operators of a formal language, defined by means of a truth theory, are no better defined than those of the natural language in which they are (ultimately) defined—at least, they are no better defined than the natural language connectives and operators which occur in the specifications of truth conditions.

How then does a person understand the connectives and operators of a natural language? In particular, how does a *mono-lingual* person understand them? Clearly, he has no metalanguage in which he can express a truth theory for his language, and a reflexive truth theory is uninformative if he does not already understand the connectives and operators of his language. My view is that he comes to understand them by acquiring a belief system on the language—a belief system which has the same basic structure and dynamics as the belief systems of other competent speakers. He learns when, and under what circumstances, to assent to or to dissent from sentences of the language in which these connectives and operators occur. And when he has mastered this, he understands them as well as they can be understood. There is nothing else to understand.

A truth theory for a language defines one language relative to another in which the connectives and operators can be presumed to be sufficiently well understood. A reflexive truth theory defines a language relative to itself. Therefore, a monolingual person's understanding of the connectives and operators of his own language cannot be derived from his acceptance of any truth theory for his language. But a monolingual person does normally understand the connectives and operators of his own language. Therefore, his understanding the connectives and operators of his language cannot in general be derived from his knowing the truth conditions for sentences in which they occur. If a monolingual person accepts all sentences of the form

'α' is true iff α

in a reflexive truth theory, then this is weak evidence that he understands "is true" and "iff" as we do. It is weak, however, because it is compatible with his understanding "is true" as meaning what we mean by "is false" and "iff" as meaning "iff it is not the case that". To decide whether he understands these terms as we do, we should have to look much further afield at his whole system of beliefs to see whether it has the relevant structural properties of a belief system on English. If it lacks these properties, then it is not a belief system on English. And this is so, even if the belief system includes what competent speakers would consider to be an adequate reflexive truth theory for the language. That someone assents to the sentences which comprise an adequate reflexive truth theory for English does not entail that he understands the sentences of English as we do.

These are the main reasons why I find traditional semantics philosophically unsatisfactory. Alternatively, I would say that to define the connectives and operators of a formal language it is sufficient to specify the relevant patterns of acceptance and rejection which would be displayed by any rational belief system on it. It will be seen that such a specification is sufficient in the sense that it enables us to derive all of the tautologies of the language and to prove consistency and completeness theorems for the logical system. It is also sufficient in the sense that it defines the connectives and operators of the formal language at least as well as such connectives and operators are defined for natural languages. And a truth theory for a formal language cannot do any better than this. It has the advantage over classical semantics of allowing us to define formal languages, the connectives and operators of which are not truth functionally definable, and it does not import into the foundations of logic or our theory of rationality the philosophically dubious notion of truth. Moreover, the theory of rational belief systems can be applied even where not every or even no belief expressible in the language is considered to be objectively true or false. One does not need to be an ethical objectivist to believe that there are valid arguments in ethics, but one does need to be an ethical objectivist to believe that moral judgements have truth values, and hence to believe that ethical arguments are classically valid or invalid. Nor does one need to believe that probability judgements are objectively true or false to believe that there are valid arguments involving probability claims.[7]

2. New Foundations for Logical Systems

Classical semantics is seen to be attractive as a foundation for logical systems for several reasons. First, it ties in well with a foundationalist epistemology. If one thinks, as most empiricists thought in the 1930's, that science is a logical structure erected upon a foundation of observation statements, that the truth or falsity of such statements is directly knowable, and that there is a language we may use to report our observations, our understanding of which is independent of any theories we may hold about the world, then classical semantics offers us a way of explaining the empirical significance of the laws and theoretical statements of science. To understand them would be to know their empirical truth conditions as they would be expressed in a theoretically neutral observation language.[9]

The importance of classical semantics for this programme is that it defines the logical connectives and operators of a language in a way which enables us to say, precisely, in terms of the most elementary sentences or predicates of the language, under what conditions a given sentence is true or false. Hence, the problem of the empirical significance of complex sentences of the language is reduced to that of the significance of its most elementary sentences and predicates.[10] And if these can be defined in terms of theoretically neutral observational sentences and predicates, then the general problem of empirical significance has been solved—provided, of course, that the language with which we began is adequate for the purposes of science.

This programme has now been abandoned by many philosophers of science, who see a far more complex interrelationship between theory and observation.[11] But it remains alive amongst philosophical logicians who hope and believe that a first order predicate language will prove to be adequate for all of the purposes of science, and who consider a truth theory for a language to be a sophisticated theory of meaning for the sentences of that language.[12] Many such philosophical logicians would no doubt deny that the old logical empiricist programme of explaining the meaning of complex theoretical statements in observational terms has any relevance to their view that an extensional language must ultimately be adequate for science. They make no explicit requirement that the primitive predicates occurring in the metalanguage, in which the truth theory for the projected extensional language of science is ultimately expressed, be observational. But their practice suggests otherwise.[13] For, while they would accept that " 'Snow is white' is true iff snow is white" may be an adequate statement of the truth conditions for this sentence, they would not consider " 'Lightning causes thunder' is true iff lightning causes thunder" to be a sufficient analysis.

A second reason why classical semantics has seemed attractive to many empiricists is that it goes hand in hand with scientific realism.[14] If truth conditions for the statements of science can be specified in a metalanguage, and each predicate of the metalanguage is such that the question of whether a given object or ordered sequence of objects satisfies this predicate is a question which can, in principle, be resolved objectively and independently of any theories one may hold about the world, then the question of the truth or falsity of the statements of science is similarly objective. It may not be resolvable—except perhaps negatively—but there should be no doubt that the statements of science at least purport to be true statements about the way things are.

I understand scientific realism to be the view that the theoretical statements of science are, or purport to be, true generalized descriptions of reality.[15] But for two reasons I find this view untenable. First, all of the most fundamental laws of science, construed as universally generalized material conditionals, are at best only vacuously true. "The total energy of every closed and isolated system remains constant." "In every inertial system the velocity of light in a vacuum is the same for all observers." "Every body not acted upon by a force continues in its state of rest or uniform motion in a straight line." "For every ideal incompressible fluid in steady flow in a uniform gravitational field the sum of the pressure head, velocity head and height h is a constant." And so far no one has been able to provide logical empiricist analyses of these statements which would show them to be more than vacuously true. The view therefore lacks empirical support, and if it is nevertheless held by most empiricists, then it is an unsupported dogma of empiricism.

Second, while I accept science as providing the best way of *understanding* the world, I am hesitant to attribute truth or falsity to some of the abstract principles required for such understanding.[16] I find the concept of truth troublesome in this context. I would be less troubled by it, if I thought there were any good reasons to believe that there is a unique and objectively best way of understanding the world. But quite apart from this hesitation, I have some general worries about the classical or absolute concept of truth. I can make some physical sense of a concept of truth which applies to a belief state of some physical system such as a brain. If a belief state of mine is true, it is presumably in virtue of some kind of correspondence relationship between what exists in my head and what exists in the rest of the physical world (including my head). But until we know a great deal more about how our brains are encoded, I do not think we can say much about such a physical concept of truth.[17] Metaphysical concepts of truth, relating such abstract third world entities as sentences or propositions to reality are all to be rejected. Such entities have no place in a severe scientific ontology.[18]

A third feature of classical semantics which has seemed attractive is that it divorces logic from psychology and epistemology. As validity of argument is classically defined an argument is valid iff there is no possible world (or alternatively, no interpretation of its non-logical terms) in which its premises are true and its conclusion false. Accordingly, whether an argument is valid or not is an *a priori* question. It depends only upon what possible worlds (or interpretations) exist, which is thought to be an *a priori* matter. But as validity is here understood, an argument is valid iff there is no rational belief system in which its premises are accepted and its conclusion rejected. Thus, for me, validity is an epistemic notion. It is a concept definable within a theory of rational belief systems. And a theory of rational belief systems is a theory designed to account for the structure of ordinary human belief systems, which is to be judged in the same kind of way as other empirical theories.

The reason the divorce has seemed attractive is that it separates questions of logic from questions about how people think or should think, which are psychological or practical questions, and turns logic into a wholly *a priori* science. This is attractive to traditional empiricists, because they have always made a sharp distinction between the empirical and the *a priori* sciences.[19] The truths of the former depend on how the world is. The truths of the latter depend on nothing more than definitions, or the conventions of language. But to modern empiricists, who reject the analytic-synthetic distinction,[20] and for whom definitions are just postulates, adopted provisionally, to be revised or rejected if this is required to develop a better theory,[21] the distinction is anachronistic. Logic should turn out to be an empirical science of some kind, which, like any other, is open to revision in the light of experience.[22]

The classical concept of validity of argument gives rise to the programme of logical analysis. For, it follows from the classical concept that to understand any statement sufficiently for all of the purposes of logic we need to know in what possible worlds (or alternatively, under what interpretations of its non-logical terms) it is true or false. My concept of validity gives rise to a new programme. For it follows from my requirements on validity that to understand any statement sufficiently for all of the purposes of logic we need to know its acceptability conditions, i.e., the conditions under which it may be accepted or rejected by an ideally rational man.

3. *Sentential Calculus*

In Chapter I, I defined the language L_0 as a language with the syntactic structure of the sentential calculus (SC), a rational belief system B on which satisfies the following requirements:

C1.   Just one of $T\alpha$, $F\alpha$ and $X\alpha$ occurs in B

C2. α and $\sim\alpha$ do not occur with the same T or F evaluation in B

C3.   (a) $T(\alpha\vee\beta)$ occurs in B only if $F\alpha$ and $F\beta$ do not both occur in B

(b) $F(\alpha\vee\beta)$ occurs in B only if neither $T\alpha$ nor $T\beta$ occurs in B

C4. (a) $T(\alpha \wedge \beta)$ occurs in B only if neither $F\alpha$ nor $F\beta$ occurs in B

(b) $F(\alpha \wedge \beta)$ occurs in B only if $T\alpha$ and $T\beta$ do not both occur in B

C5. (a) $T(\alpha \supset \beta)$ occurs in B only if $T\alpha$ and $F\beta$ do not both occur in B

(b) $F(\alpha \supset \beta)$ occurs in B only if neither $F\alpha$ nor $T\beta$ occurs in B

C6. (a) $T(\alpha \equiv \beta)$ occurs in B only if α and β do not occur with opposite T or F evaluations in B

(b) $F(\alpha \equiv \beta)$ occurs in B only if α and β do not occur with the same T or F evaluation in B.

C7. B is completable through every extension of L_0.

In saying that L_0 has the syntactic structure of SC, I mean only that α is a sentence of L_0 iff α is a *wff* of SC. The tautologies of L_0 are those sentences of L_0 which do not occur with an F evaluation in any rational belief system on L_0. It is demonstrable that the tautologies of L_0 are just the valid *wffs* of SC.

The requirements C1 and C7 are general rationality requirements. C2 to C6 are specific requirements which implicitly define the logical connectives and operators of L_0. The operators '$\sim$', '$\vee$', '$\wedge$', '$\supset$' and '$\equiv$' are intended to be formal analogues of the sentential negation, disjunction, conjunction, conditional and biconditional operators of natural languages. They are intended to be such in the way in which the mass-points of Newtonian physics are intended to be the formal analogues of physical particles. It is not a requirement on a formal analogue of anything that it should have just the same properties. Idealization is always involved in the processes of theory construction. But it is not the case that any idealization is as good as any other. The test of a theory, and hence of the idealizations upon which it is founded, lies in the viability of the research programme which it generates. If the differences between, say, "and" and '$\wedge$' can all be attributed to implications which hold only in special circumstances—contextual implications, conversational implicatures, etc.—then '$\wedge$' may be a satisfactory formal analogue of the natural language conjunction. Whether '$\supset$' and '$\equiv$' are satisfactory formal analogues of the natural language connectives "if ... then ..." and "if and only if" will be discussed in Chapter III. The requirements C5(b) and C6(b) are, perhaps, counterintuitive. Possible alternatives to them will be discussed in Chapter III.

It should be noted that the requirements C1 to C7 on a rational belief system B on L_0 are very weak. They forbid $F(\alpha \vee \sim\alpha)$ occurring in B, but do not require $T(\alpha \vee \sim\alpha)$ to occur. They forbid $T\alpha$, $T(\alpha \supset \beta)$ and $F\beta$ all occurring in B, but they do not require that if $T\alpha$ and $T(\alpha \supset \beta)$ both occur in B, then $T\beta$ also occurs in B. This does not matter very much if we choose to define a tautology of a language L as any sentence of L which does not occur with an F evaluation on any rational belief system on L. But the weakness of these requirements may be seen as an objection. To overcome this difficulty we might propose the following *strict rationality* requirement. A belief system B on L is strictly rational iff B is rational, and

(1) $T\alpha$ occurs in B if $F\alpha$ does not occur in any completed extension of B on any extension of L

(2) $F\alpha$ occurs in B if $T\alpha$ does not occur in any completed extension of B on any extension of L.

Given this requirement, we could define a tautology of L as any sentence of L which has a T evaluation in every strictly rational belief system on L. However, strictly rational belief systems are really only for the gods, and they have no need for a system of logic anyway. Therefore, I prefer the weaker concept of rationality, and the corresponding definition of tautologousness.

4. *The Modal Sentential Calculi*

In general, a possibility claim is a claim that something is compatible with something else. The particular kind of possibility claim we are dealing with depends on what that something else is said to be. If 'α' is compatible with *all tautologies*, then 'α' is *logically* possible. If 'α' is compatible with *the laws of nature* then 'α' is *physically* possible. If 'α' is compatible with *the established facts of history*, then 'α' is *historically* possible.[23] If 'α' is compatible with *what is universally acknowledged*, then 'α' is possible in some other sense.

To say that 'α' is compatible with 'β' is to say that $T\alpha$ and $T\beta$ both occur in some rational belief system on the language. Hence to claim that it is possible that α, in the sense of, say, physical possibility, is to say that there is a rational belief system on the language, or on some extension of the language, in which $T\alpha$ occurs and in which every law of nature occurs with a T evaluation. Hence for this sense of possibility, $T\Diamond\alpha$ occurs in a rational belief system B only if $T\alpha$ occurs in some completed extension (perhaps on some extension of the language) of some belief system B' which contains *all and only* those beliefs which are thought to express laws of nature.

The claim that it is impossible that α is similarly the claim that 'α' is incompatible with something else. Let B' be a belief system which contains just what some individual A considers to be historically well established. Let '$\Diamond$' be the historical possibility operator. Then if A's belief system B is rational, then $F\Diamond\alpha$ occurs in B only if $T\alpha$ does not occur in any completed extension of B' through any extension of the language. Moreover, since the members of B' are members of B, B is an extension of B', and, therefore, $F\Diamond\alpha$ occurs in B only if $T\alpha$ does not occur in any completed extension of B.

Let $E(B')$ be the set of all completed extensions of B', where B' is defined in relation to B for some specified sense of "possibility". Then we may say that if B is rational, then

C8*　　(a)　$T\Diamond\alpha$ occurs in B, only if $T\alpha$ occurs in some member of $E(B')$.

　　　　(b)　$F\Diamond\alpha$ occurs in B, only if $F\alpha$ occurs in B.

The requirement C8*(b) is apparently stronger than the requirement that $F\Diamond\alpha$ occurs in B only if $T\alpha$ does not occur in any completed extension of B. But in fact, given the general rationality requirement of completability, they are equivalent.

The claim, that it is not necessarily true that α, is the claim that it is possible that it is not the case that α, and the claim, that it is necessarily true that α, is the claim that it is impossible that not-α. Therefore, we may say that if B is rational, then

C9*　　$\Box\alpha$ and $\Diamond\sim\alpha$ do not occur with the same T or F evaluation in B.

It is traditional to make the necessity operator primitive, and to define the possibility operator. I shall follow this practice here. Accordingly, I propose the following requirements on the structure of any rational belief system B on any language which includes necessity and possibility operators:

C8.　　(a)　$T\Box\alpha$ occurs in B only if $T\alpha$ occurs in B

　　　　(b)　$F\Box\alpha$ occurs in B only if $F\alpha$ occurs in some member of $E(B')$

C9.　　$\Diamond\alpha$ and $\Box\sim\alpha$ do not occur with the same T or F evaluations in B.

The two sets of requirements C8* and C9*, and C8 and C9 are equivalent. In these requirements, B' is a belief system which is to be defined in some way in relation to B, and $E(B')$ is the set of all completed extensions of B' on all extensions of the language.

The requirements C8 and C9 do not determine unique senses of "necessity" or "possibility" or even a unique logic of necessity and possibility claims. The logical system we obtain from this semantics depends on how B' is defined in relation to B. Any language L, a rational belief system B on which satisfies the requirements C8 and C9, may be called a *modal language*. And if this language L has the syntactic structure of the modal sentential calculi, i.e., if α is a sentence of L iff α is a *wff* of, say, S5, then L may be called a *modal sentential language*. The theorems of the various modal sentential calculi are the tautologies of appropriate modal sentential languages. Here we shall consider only the four principal modal sentential languages, MT, MB, M4 and M5, the tautologies of which are the theorems of the modal logical systems T, B, S4 and S5, respectively.[24]

For each of the principal modal sentential languages, $X\alpha$ is a member of B' unless the requirements on B' determine otherwise. The requirements on B' are some combination of the following:

N1. $T\alpha \in B'$, if $T\Box\alpha \in B$
N2. $T\Diamond\alpha \in B'$, if $T\alpha \in B$
N3. $T\Box\alpha \in B'$, if $T\Box\alpha \in B$
N4. $T\Diamond\alpha \in B'$, if $T\Diamond\alpha \in B$.

N1 is a requirement on B' for all of the principal modal sentential languages. For MT, it is the only requirement. For MB, the requirements are N1 and N2. For M4, they are N1 and N3. And for M5, they are N1, N2 and N3, or alternatively, just N1 and N4.

It is debatable what should be included in B'. The analysis suggests that, for physical and historical possibility and necessity claims, even the requirement N1 may be too strong. For it suggests that $T\alpha$ should occur in B' *only if* α is considered to express a law of nature, or an historically well established fact, as the case may be. But statements about what is physically or historically necessary, non-necessary, possible or impossible will not themselves be laws of nature or historically well established facts. A weaker requirement on B' therefore seems to be required, and one suggested by the analysis is

N5. $T\alpha \in B'$ if α is a sentence of L_0 and $T\square\alpha \in B$.

For a modal language for which this was the only requirement on B', iterated and nested modalities would be of little interest. It would be preferable, therefore, and would achieve the intended result, if we were to retain the requirement N1 on B', and change the syntax of the language so as to exclude all iterated and nested modalities. I have elsewhere called this restricted language MO.1.[25] The tautologies of MO.1 are just the theorems of zero or first order modality of all standard modal logical systems, i.e., the logical system SO.1.

However, I am now convinced that the restriction to at most first order modalities is not required. For the logical necessity and possibility operators there is no justification for the restriction. A statement about what is logically necessary, non-necessary, possible or impossible in a language of zero-order modality will be a statement in a language of first-order modality; and such first-order modality statements may themselves be the subject of logical necessity, non-necessity, possibility and impossibility claims in a language of second-order modality, and so on. Moreover, the restriction is unnecessary, even where no logical modalities are involved. Let 'α' be any sentence of L_0. Then to say that it is physically possible that α is just to say that it is compatible with the laws of nature that it is physically possible that α. And while this may be an odd thing to say, it is certainly intelligible. For this sense of "possibility", $T\diamond\diamond\alpha$ occurs in a rational belief system B_2 on a second-order modal language L_2 only if $T\diamond\alpha$ occurs in some rational belief system on a first-order modal language L_1 in which the set of beliefs concerning the laws of nature is the same as in B_2.

Let L_0, L_1, L_2, ... L_ω be a series of languages, beginning with the base language L_0, and such that

(a) If α is a sentence of L_n, then α, $\square\alpha$ and $\diamond\alpha$ are sentences of L_{n+1}

(b) If α is a sentence of L_{n+1}, then $\sim\alpha$ is a sentence of L_{n+1}

(c) If α and β are sentences of L_{n+1}, and $*$ is any logical connective of L_0, then $\alpha*\beta$ is a sentence of L_{n+1}.

The language L_n is a language of nth-order modality. The sentences of L_0 are the wffs of SC, and those of L_ω are those of any standard modal sentential calculus. We may assume, for the present, that the language L_0 is adequate for expressing all of our first-order beliefs. Let B_0 be our belief system on L_0. The language

L_1 is adequate for expressing our basic beliefs as well as certain meta-beliefs about the structure of B_0. Let B_1 be our belief system on L_1. If B_1 is rational, then $T\Box\alpha_1 \in B_1$ only if $T\alpha \in B_0$, $F\Box\alpha \in B_1$ only if $F\alpha$ occurs in some member of $E(B_0')$, $\Diamond\alpha$ and $\Box\sim\alpha$ do not occur with the same T or F evaluation in B_1, and if $T\alpha$, $F\alpha$ or $X\alpha$ occurs in B_0, then $T\alpha$, $F\alpha$ or $X\alpha$, as the case may be, occurs in B_1. The belief system B_1 thus includes B_0, and no extra first-order beliefs; but it also includes certain meta-beliefs about the structure of B_0. Which meta-beliefs are included in B_1 depends upon the relationship between B_0 and B_0'. Until we know what senses of "necessity" and "possibility" we are dealing with, we cannot say anything more about this relationship than that B_0 is an extension of B_0'.

The language L_2 is adequate for expressing not only what is contained in B_1, but also certain meta-beliefs about the structure of B_1. Let B_2 be our belief system on L_2. Then, assuming that the second-order modalities have the same sense as the first order ones, B_2 should not contain any zero or first-order modality claims which are not already included in B_1, or fail to include any which are. Hence B_2 may differ from B_1 only in that it may contain some second-order modality claims which are not included in B_1. B_2 should be just an extension into a second-order modal language of B_1.

Let "α_1" be any sentence of L_1 of first-order modality. Then, if B_2 is rational, $T\Box\alpha_1$ occurs in B_2 only if $T\alpha_1$ occurs in B_1 (and hence in B_2), and $F\Box\alpha_1$ occurs in B_2 only if $F\alpha_1$ occurs in some rational belief system B on L_1 in which the modalities are defined relative to B_0'. It is not hard to show that if $T\Diamond\alpha$ occurs in some such rational belief system on L_1, then $F\Diamond\alpha$ does not occur in any such rational belief system on L_1. Hence, if $T\Diamond\alpha$ occurs in B_1 (and therefore in B_2), then $F\Box\Diamond\alpha$ does not occur in B_2. Therefore, if the second order modalities in L_2 all have the same sense as the primary modalities in L_1, then

$$\Diamond\alpha \supset \Box\Diamond\alpha$$

is a tautology of L_2. If all higher order modalities in L_ω have the same sense as the primary ones, then the tautologies of L_ω are the theorems of S5.

5. First-Order Predicate Calculus

On the classical view, validity is basically a property of *sentence schemata*. A sentence schema is valid iff it is true on all interpretations. A *sentence*, by contrast, can be said to be valid only in a derivative sense. It is valid iff it is an instance of a valid sentence schema. For this derivative sense of "validity" some other term such as "logical truth" or "tautology" is often used. A realist about possible worlds could, but seldom does, take a very different view of the matter. For there is no reason why he should not consider the concept of validity applicable to sentences to be the fundamental one. Thus, he could say that a sentence is valid if it is *true in all possible worlds*. And then, if he wished to speak of the validity of sentence schemata, he could define a valid sentence schema as one, all instances of which (in the language, and in all extensions of the language) are valid. My concept of validity for sentences is conceptually closer to this "possible worlds" concept. For me, a sentence is valid, or as I prefer to say, *tautologous*, iff there is no *rational* belief system on the language in which it occurs with an *F*-evaluation. Alternatively, I could say that a tautology of a language is any sentence which occurs with a *T*-evaluation in every *strictly rational* belief system on the language. Or again, I could say that a tautology is a sentence which occurs with a *T*-evaluation in every *completed rational belief system* on the language or on any extension of the language. Finally, if the assumptions are made that

(a) Every completed rational belief system truly describes some possible world, and

(b) Every possible world is truly described by some completed rational belief system,

then I could say that a sentence is a tautology iff it is true in all possible worlds.

The language in which first-order predicate calculus, LPC, is formulated contains both open and closed sentence schemata. In the formal language, LP, shortly to be described, a *sentence* of LP is any *closed sentence schema* of LPC with individual constants—there being no open sentences in LP. It may be said, therefore that what I am here calling a sentence, everyone else would call a sentence schema, and hence that my concept of validity does not apply directly to the sentences of LP, but only to the sentences of some natural language for which the terms and predicates of LP might be dummies. My objection to saying this is that it misrepresents what I am trying to do. For, I do not regard the predicates and individual constants of LP as *dummies* for the predicates and names of any natural language—any more than I regard the point—masses of particle dynamics as dummies for, say, protons and electrons. Rather, I regard them as constituents of an idealized language which can be used in the theory of rational belief systems as a *model* for natural languages. Accordingly, I would define a tautology of LP in exactly the same way as I would define a tautology of any natural language, viz., as any sentences of the language which does not occur with an F evaluation in any rational belief system on the language.

The language LP contains a finite, or at most a denumerable infinity of terms or individual constants a_1, a_2, ... b_1, b_2, ... c_1, c_2, ..., one-place predicates F_1, F_2, ... G_1, G_2, ... H_1, H_2, ... two-place predicates F_1', F_2', ... G_1', G_2', ... H_1', H_2', ... and so on, a denumerable infinity of individual variables x_1, x_2, ... y_1, y_2, ... z_1, z_2, ..., the universal and existential quantifiers, $\forall$ and $\exists$, and the sentences, connectives and operators of L_0. To avoid difficulties arising from empty names I assume that every competent speaker of LP considers every term of LP to have reference. For a language with empty names we should need also to have an existence predicate E, and to modify appropriately the rationality requirements on belief systems on the language.[26]

The requirements on a rational belief system B on LP include C1 to C7 as well as the following:

C10   (a) $T\forall x\alpha$ occurs in B only if no instantiation of $\forall x\alpha$ occurs with an F evaluation in B

         (b) $F\forall x\alpha$ occurs in B only if some instantiation of $\forall x\alpha$ occurs with an F evaluation in some member of $E(B)$.

C11   (a) $T\exists x\alpha$ occurs in B only if some instantiation of $\forall x\alpha$ occurs with a T evaluation in some member of $E(B)$

         (b) $F\exists x\alpha$ occurs in B only if no instantiation of $\exists x\alpha$ occurs with a T evaluation in B.

In these requirements $E(B)$ is the set of all completed extensions of B on all extensions of LP. The requirements C10(a) and C11(b) seem evident enough. If a person's belief system systematically violated either of these requirements we should have good reason to suppose that he did not understand the universal or existential quantifier of the language. The requirements C10(b) and C11(a) may need some explanation. If someone holds the belief $F\forall x\alpha$, but there is no rational way of extending his belief system so that it should include a falsity claim on some instantiation of $\forall x\alpha$, then either he holds the belief irrationally for some reason (e.g., because his belief system is not in equilibrium under all pressures of internal criticism and discussion), or he does not understand the universal quantifier of the language. Similarly, if someone holds the belief $T \exists x\alpha$, but there is no rational way of extending his belief system so that it includes a truth claim on some instantiation of $\exists x\alpha$, then again, he either holds the belief irrationally, or he does not understand the existential quantifier.

The requirements C1 to C7, C10 and C11 are a sufficient basis for the first-order predicate calculus. That is, every valid closed sentence schema of LPC is an LP tautology, and conversely. Proofs of soundness and completeness can be constructed along standard lines, since every completed belief system defines a standard valuation, and conversely. Moreover, since the rationality requirements include completability through all extensions of the language, the system is strongly complete.

The proofs are formally analogous to those developed on the sophisticated substitutional interpretation of the quantifiers. But it should be noted that the theory of quantification implied in my analysis, while substitutional in spirit, cannot strictly be classified as either objectual or substitutional. For *these are categories which belong to a different programme of analysis.* Truth conditions for the sentences of LP are nowhere offered, and the basis for predicate calculus suggested here is independent of any theory of truth. A theory of quantification is substitutional if it offers the following kind of analysis: "$\forall x\alpha$" is true iff every substitution instance of "$\forall x\alpha$" is true. It is objectual if the analysis offered is equivalent to the claim that "$\forall x\alpha$" is true in a given domain iff 'α' is true of every object x in that domain. Since I do not need to accept either analysis, my account is neutral between the objectual and substitutional interpretations of the quantifiers. Rational belief systems on languages which included the quantifiers would have to satisfy my requirements whatever account of the truth conditions of statements made using the quantifiers might be given.

6. *Other Developments*

It is fairly clear what further developments are possible. A language for second-order predicate calculus may be constructed by introducing a denumerable infinity of n-adic predicate variables into the language structure of LP, and making requirements formally analogous to C10 and C11 on $\forall\theta\alpha$ and $\exists\theta\alpha$ (where θ is any n-adic predicate variable). Let this second order predicate language be LP2. Then axioms formally analogous to those required for LP are provable for LP2. Moreover, since the account of quantification which I have offered is independent of any interpretation of the quantifiers as objectual or substitutional, I do not need to admit either properties or universals as items in my ontology—not that I would mind doing so.

For a non-modal predicate language with identity we may introduce a two-place predicate constant 'I' into the base language (LP or LP2). A rational belief system B on LP$+I$, for example, should satisfy the requirements C1 to C7, C10 and C11, and

C12   (a) $TIab$ occurs in B only if no two sentences $\alpha(a)$ and $\alpha(b)$ of LP$+I$ such that $\alpha(b)$ contains b in one or more places in which $\alpha(a)$ contains a occur with opposite T of F evaluations in B.

(b) $FIab$ occurs in B only if there are two sentences $\alpha(a)$ and $\alpha(b)$ related to each other as in C12 (a) which occur with opposite T or F evaluations in some completable extension of B on some extension of LP$+I$.

In place of "Iab" we may write "$a = b$", in accordance with normal practice, and the usual theorems

$a = a$

and

$(a = b) \supset (\alpha(a) \supset \alpha(b))$

are readily provable.

The requirements C12(a) and (b) need some discussion. If someone thinks it is true that $a = b$ and that $\alpha(a)$, but thinks it false that $\alpha(b)$, then we have good reason to suppose that he does not understand the predicate '$=$'. At least, this is so for the simple language LP$+I$. It is not true for certain richer languages which contain demonstratives such as "that" in "John believes that $a = a$" or the quotation marks in "John says "a is a horse"".[27] For in such languages, the term 'a' may occur in a sentence not as a referring expression but as (part of) the object of reference. Nor is it true for modal predicate languages—although for a different reason.

Belief systems on modal languages are built up recursively from belief systems on non-modal languages. If B_0 is a belief system on a non-modal language such as L_0, LP, LP2 or LP$+I$, and B_0 contains a set of knowledge claims K_0 (i.e., sentences which occur in B_0 with T or F evaluations), then one selects some subset K_0' of B_0 as objects of necessity or impossibility claims—the selection made depending upon the particular modalities we are dealing with. These new beliefs are beliefs concerning the epistemic status of the elements of the original belief system B_0, and these meta-beliefs are expressible in a language L_1 which contains first-order modalities. Let B_1 be the belief system on L_1 thus derived from the belief system B_0 on the original non-modal language. Then the process can be repeated to obtain a belief system B_2 on a second-order modal language which includes certain meta-beliefs about the belief system B_1, and so on.

Now suppose that $T\alpha(a)$ and $T(a=b)$ both occur in B_0. Then if B_0 is completable, $F\alpha(b)$ does not also occur in B_0. But in the process of modal escalation, there is no requirement that if $T\square\alpha(a)$ occurs in B_1, $T\square(a=b)$ also occurs in B_1. Hence there is no reason why B_1 should not include both $T\square\alpha(a)$ and $F\square\alpha(b)$. Therefore, for belief systems on modal predicate languages, the requirements C12(a) and (b) cannot be generalized. Identity must be defined relative to the base language.

The modal predicate languages with identity do not therefore contain the usual paradoxes. In particular, neither

$$(a=b) \supset \square(a=b)$$

nor

$$(a\neq b) \supset \square(a\neq b)$$

is a tautology of any of them. To derive either of these as tautologies, we should have to consider $\square(\ldots=\ldots)$ to be a predicate of some extension of LP. But '$\square$' is here understood to be a sentence forming operator on sentences, not as a predicate forming operator on predicates. To assert that a is necessarily identical to b is not to assert that a bears a relationship of *necessary identity* to b. It is just to assert that a is identical to b, and at the same time to express one's meta-belief that the non-identity of a and b is incompatible with all tautologies, or laws of nature, or whatever.

To forestall a possible objection, it should be noted that there is no contradiction between this conception of the modal operators, and the occurrence in modal predicate languages of sentences of the form "$\forall x\square\alpha$" or others in which a modality occurs within the scope of a quantifier and includes within its scope a variable bound by that quantifier. For quantified sentences are here derived from closed sentences by existential or universal generalization (rather than by closure of open sentences) and the acceptability of quantified sentences depends in various ways upon the acceptability of their instantiations. Thus, $T\forall x\square\alpha$ can only occur in a belief system B on a modal predicate language L if no instantiation of $\forall x\square\alpha$ occurs with an F evaluation in B, and $F\forall x\square\alpha$ can only occur in B if some instantiation of $\forall x\square\alpha$ occurs with an F evaluation in some extension of B on some extension of L. $\forall x\square\alpha$ is, therefore, just a universal generalization of a *de dicto* modality claim, and no independent account of modalities as operators on open sentences is required.

The various modal predicate languages have the properties we should expect them to have. The tautologies of $LP+MT$ are the closed valid *wffs* of $LPC+T$; the tautologies of $LP+MB+I$ are the closed valid wffs of $LPC+B+CI$; and so on. Every instance of the converse of the Barcan Formula is a tautology of $LP+MT$, but instances of the Barcan Formula itself, viz.

$$\forall x\square\alpha \supset \square\forall x\alpha$$

are not, in general, tautologies of this language. It is well known that the Barcan Formula may be added as an axiom schema to $LPC+T$ to yield to modal predicate calculus $LPC+T+BF$. To obtain a semantics for this system we require the assumption that there is an extension LP^* of LP which is an extension of every extension of LP. However, the requirement that a belief system on $LP+MT$ be completable through to LP^*+MT, supposing there to be such a language, is not very plausible as a rationality requirement.

7. Logic and Psychology

My aim in this chapter has been to argue that the laws of logic are the laws of rational thought. The theorems of all standard logical systems are the tautologies of simple formal languages which can be defined by specifying certain primitive requirements on the structure of rational belief systems upon them. The formal languages are to be understood as models for natural languages chosen for the purpose of representing certain general features of these languages. The laws governing the structure of rational belief systems on formal languages are to be understood as laws applicable to belief systems on natural languages in the kind of way that the laws of physics are to be understood as laws applicable to natural physical systems. Not every belief system will be rational in the sense that it has all of the structural features of the idealized belief systems. But then, not every physical system, and maybe even no physical system, will have all of the characteristics of the idealized systems of physical theory with reference to which the laws of physics are formulated.

What is important, and what makes *conventionalism* an untenable position concerning physical theory, is that a good physical theory must generate a viable research programme. It is not to be expected—indeed, it is often absurd to expect—natural physical systems to behave like their idealized counterparts in physical theory. But insofar as they do not behave in this way, we have what is to be regarded as *an effect*. For, in general, an effect is just a difference between actual behaviour, and some kind of idealized behaviour. The viability of the research programme generated by a theory depends upon the ability of researchers to discover adequate explanations for these effects, i.e., differences between actual and theoretical behaviour. Similarly, what makes conventionalism an untenable position concerning the theory of the structure of rational belief systems is that it too must generate a viable research programme. Insofar as natural belief systems are not rational according to the intended interpretations of the theoretical models, we have effects for which explanations are required. The adequacy of any theory of rational belief systems must depend upon the ability of researchers to discover satisfactory explanations for these effects. In the following chapter,[28] I will discuss what appears to be a serious discrepancy between my theoretical structure for rational belief systems on languages with conditionals and the actual structure of human belief systems on natural languages with such connectives.

If my view of the nature of logical theory is correct, then the laws of belief are the laws of thought, and logic is a branch of psychology. This is an old-fashioned view, sometimes known as psychologism,[29] which has long been out of favour. But I know of no good arguments against it. By "psychologism," I do not mean the doctrine, which Popper is so much against, and which he discusses in relation to Fries' trilemma, that the basic statements of science are *justified* by experience.[30] I mean that older doctrine to which he refers when he says that it was not so long ago that logic was held to be "a science dealing with mental processes and their laws—the laws of our thought".[31] And one can surely hold this view without holding that any of our basic judgements about validity or invalidity are *justified* by our "feelings of conviction".

Psychologism is not to be confused with *foundationalism*, which, like Popper, I reject. Nevertheless, if I am right, then Popper's distinction between the *logic* of knowledge and the *psychology* of knowledge[32] cannot be sustained.

The main objections to the view that logic is a science dealing with mental processes and their laws are:

1. Mental processes are non-physical processes occurring in people's minds which do not obey strict laws (i.e., laws of a non-statistical character). But the laws of logic are strict and therefore not laws of thought.

   My reply is that mental processes are physical processes occurring in people's heads which are every bit as deterministic as physical processes which occur elsewhere in nature. The objectivity of logic, and the strictness of its laws is evidence for this. To explain this objectivity and strictness I would postulate that human beings are genetically determined to think in certain sorts of ways—in ways which presumably have survival value for the human species.

2. No one is fully rational according to the ideals of rationality which I have postulated. People contradict themselves. Therefore, if the laws of logic are laws about how people think, then they are all false.

   This objection rests upon a naive view about the nature of scientific laws. Scientific laws are not universal generalizations like "All crows are black", but statements about how certain kinds of idealized entities would behave under certain idealized conditions. They are principles determining some ideal of physical behaviour with which actual behaviour is to be compared and explained. The principles of logic are like this.

NOTES

1. I have in mind a procedure like the one followed by McKinsey, Sugar and Suppes (1953) in constructing an axiomatic foundation for classical mechanics.

2. See Quine (1969), p. 146.

3. See Lewis (1973), Ch. 4.

4. My reasons for thinking the programme to have been largely unsuccessful are set out in some detail in Ellis (1969).

5. At the end of his paper, Davidson (1967) lists a number of other problems which have so far not been solved. But where are the achievements which would justify confidence that the programme is worth pursuing? There is Russell's theory of definite descriptions. Is there anything else?

6. See Davidson (1967), p. 7. Davidson here uses the word "meaning" where older empiricists would have used the phrase "empirical significance". For him, the semantical concept of truth is "a sophisticated and powerful foundation for a competent theory of meaning", and "To know the semantic concept of truth for a language is to know what it is for a sentence—any sentence—to be true, and this amounts, in one good sense we can give to the phrase, to understanding the language. In his more recent writings, however, Davidson has rejected the idea that a truth theory is, by itself, a theory of meaning. See Davidson, (1973).

7. I do not mean this analogy to be taken too seriously. A sentence is not a name or an expression which *refers* to a bearer of truth or falsity—although it may be exhibited for this purpose.

8. Subjectivists, like de Finetti (1937) and Savage (1961), do not believe that subjective probability judgements are objectively true or false. Nevertheless, they believe that there are valid arguments involving such judgements. The argument:

It is very probable that p
It is very probable that if p then q

∴ It is very improbable that q

is an invalid argument, since a rational man who accepts its premisses must reject its conclusion. But the argument is not classically invalid if its premisses and conclusion do not have objective truth values.

9. The argument against the existence of a theoretically neutral observation language which could serve as a foundation for such an empiricist epistemology has been presented in Feyerabend (1965). If Feyerabend's conclusions are accepted, then one of the most important motivations for trying to develop classical semantics for languages adequate for the purposes of science vanishes.

10. The problem of the empirical basis of science has been discussed by many philosophers. But perhaps the best known discussions are those of Popper (1934) §7, and Feyerabend (1965). But there is a beautiful paper by Alfred Bohnen (1969) which deserves mention here. If there is any emerging consensus on this question, it is that there is no firm foundation for knowledge which could serve as basis for understanding the laws and theoretical statements of empirical science. Carnap's programme of trying to specify empirical truth conditions for the statements of science has not only failed to yield the required analyses, it would not succeed in solving the problem of empirical significance even if it did, since there would remain the problem of the empirical basis.

11. For some other recent discussions, see Lakatos and Musgrave (1970).

12. See Davidson (1967), p. 7.

13. See Davidson (1976), p. 20.

14. The kind of theory of scientific realism I have in mind is that developed at length in Smart (1963).

15. I would distinguish this concept of scientific realism from what might be called *scientific entity realism.* I have no wish to deny the reality of atoms, electrons, or other postulated *constituents* of the universe. My position is not that of Mach or Ostwald. My view is concerned with the laws of science and the idealized entities to which they (apparently) refer. The atoms and electrons are physical entities constitutive of the physical world. Science makes models of them and formulates laws governing the behaviour of these idealized particles in various idealized spaces. My position is that these laws are not to be thought of as true generalized descriptions of the behaviour of the particles of physical reality, but statements about how these particles would behave in various kinds of idealized systems if they were exactly like the idealized particles of the models.

16. I am hesitant, for example, to say of Newton's First Law of Motion that it is true or false in any absolute sense—for reasons explained at length in Ellis (1965a).

17. I have discussed this concept of truth elsewhere in Ellis (1969).

18. My ontology is one of physical entities and properties. On our present understanding of physics, I would consider a physical entity to be anything which has mass or energy. A physical event is any change in the energy distribution within the universe. A physical process is any causally connected sequence of physical events. A physical property is any property of a physical entity, possession of which makes a difference to some physical process. For a full discussion of my concept of the physical see my (1976b).

19. The distinction has been commonly accepted by empiricists since Hume. (See *Enquiry Concerning Human Understanding*, Section IV).

20. As in Quine (1953).

21. Cf. Popper (1934), p. 55.

22. The experience in this case is expressed in the intuitive judgements we make concerning the rationality (or otherwise) of holding certain combinations of beliefs. These are the facts which our logical theories must account for. It is not to be supposed that any logical theory will acount for all such facts. The most we can ask for is a theory which provides us with a framework for understanding why we make the judgements we do.

23. For a discussion of some of these concepts of possibility, see Reichenbach (1928), §7.

24. The proofs of soundness are elementary. For example, to prove the lemma that $\Box(\alpha \supset \beta) \supset (\Box\alpha \supset \Box\beta)$ is a tautology of MT, the following is sufficient. Suppose it is not a tautology. Then there is a completed rational belief system B in which $T\Box(\alpha \supset \beta)$, $T\Box\alpha$ and $F\Box\beta$ all occur. For this B, B' includes $T(\alpha \supset \beta)$ and $T\alpha$. Hence, $T\alpha$, $T(\alpha \supset \beta)$ and $T\beta$ all occur in every member of $E(B')$. But since $F\Box\beta$ occurs in B, $F\beta$ occurs in some member of $E(B')$. Hence the lemma. Similar proofs for the other axioms and rules of the various modal systems are easily constructed. The completeness proofs depend on regarding a completed belief system as a true description of a possible world, and the set of worlds accessible to a given world truly described by B as the set truly described by the members of $E(B')$. The completeness proofs are then standard.

25. See Ellis and Davidson (1976).

26. For a language with empty names we should need to have an existence predicate E, and to modify the rules to

   C10′   (a) $T\forall x\,\alpha$ occurs in B only if no instantiation of $\forall x(Ex \supset \alpha)$ occurs with an F evaluation in B.
   (b) $F\forall x\,\alpha$ occurs in B only if some instantiation of $\forall x(Ex \supset \alpha)$ occurs with an F evaluation in some member of $E(B)$.

and to have analogous rules for $\exists x\alpha$.

27. I take the view that quotation marks are demonstratives, and reject Davidson's view that a quoted sentence is an abbreviated structural description of that sentence. (See Davidson (1969a).) I do so, because Davidson's theory is unable to account for the fact that we can understand such sentences as □ is an ancient Tibetan character even though we should be hard pressed to offer a structural description of this character.

28. See Chapter III, Section 4.

29. This view had some currency in the last century. It was defended in Mill (1843) and (1865), and Lipps (1880). Lipps claimed that "Logic is the physics of thought, or it is nothing", (quoted in Chisholm (1966) p. 79). It was attacked in Husserl (1900–1) and Frege (1884).

30. Popper (1934), p. 105.

31. *Ibid.*, p. 98.

32. *Ibid.*, p. 31.

Chapter III

The Laws of Hypothetical Reasoning

Hypothetical reasoning is reasoning with conditionals, and the laws of hypothetical reasoning are those of rational belief systems on languages in which conditionals occur. The languages we have so far discussed contain only *material conditionals*, which, as we shall see, are conditionals of a rather special kind. Certainly, those conditionals known as *counterfactuals* are not material conditionals. For, if they were, they would all be true.

The three main kinds of conditionals discussed in the literature are the *material, strict* and *variably strict* conditionals. The usual semantics for these three kinds are strikingly different from each other: "$\alpha \supset \beta$" is true iff 'α' is false or 'β' is true; "$\alpha \ni \beta$" is true at world w_i iff "$\alpha \supset \beta$" is true at every world accessible to w_i; and "$\alpha \square \rightarrow \beta$" is true at world w_i iff there is a world w_j in which 'α' and 'β' are both true which is more like w_i than any world in which 'α' is true and 'β' false. On what is perhaps the most popular view, the *indicative conditionals* of English (i.e., those expressed in the *indicative mood*) are normally material conditionals, while those expressed in the subjunctive mood are usually variably strict. But the semantic differences between these two kinds of conditionals are so great that one may wonder about the connection between them.

In this chapter, I will develop a general theory of conditionals from which the various kinds of conditionals can be derived as special cases. The general theory is that a conditional of any kind "$\alpha \rightarrow \beta$" is a sentence which is accepted as true in a rational belief system B only if the belief that 'β' is false does not occur in any completed extension of a belief system B'_α which is derived from B on the supposition that α. What kind of conditional it is depends on how B'_α is defined in relation to B. According to this general theory, the semantic differences between the various kinds of conditionals are still very substantial, and the view that the indicative conditionals of English are material conditionals, while the subjunctives are variably strict, can be seen to be untenable. For, there is a much closer semantic link between an indicative conditional, and its corresponding subjunctive, than there is between any material conditional, and the corresponding variably strict one. Indeed it will be argued that, with perhaps some rare exceptions, the indicative conditionals of English, and their corresponding subjunctives, are just variant locutions for the one kind of conditional, the logic for which is variably strict. The indicative conditionals and their corresponding subjunctives will be shown to have the same acceptability conditions, but different assertability conditions.

In developing this theory of conditionals, I will try to show how it is able to cope with various general difficulties with "possible worlds" theories. Some of these difficulties simply do not arise in my theory, since I do not need to postulate the existence of any other possible worlds. Others do arise, or arise in another form, but I think I can deal with these at least as well as "possible worlds" theorists can deal with their problems.

1. *Objections to "Possible Worlds" Semantics for Counterfactuals*

A classical semantics for a language is a truth theory for that language. A "possible worlds" semantics is a truth theory in which the truth of some sentence is said to depend upon the existence of some possible world which may or may not be actual. Such semantics are not always taken seriously by logicians as truth theories, and often the possible worlds they refer to are regarded only as convenient fictions. My concern here is not with them, but with those realists about possible worlds who believe that a "possible worlds" semantics is a genuine truth theory.

My main objections to realist "possible worlds" semantics for counterfactuals are global ones. That is, they do not depend upon the details of any particular semantic theory, and they apply to any seriously intended "possible worlds" semantics for such conditionals.[1] For convenience, I will hang my objections on the Lewis' theory,[2] but what I have to say applies as well to Stalnaker's.[3] I have six such objections.

1. If a counterfactual conditional is a claim about the existence of some world more like our own than any other of a certain kind, then it is hard to see how we could ever be justified in thinking it to be true. Since different possible worlds cannot causally interact, we cannot learn about their existence, or investigate them, in any of the usual ways. Therefore, we have to suppose that we can know about them just by taking thought. But other possible worlds are not supposed to be abstract entities, like numbers, about which we might be said to have acquired knowledge just by taking thought,

but physical realms like ours, in which physical beings of various kinds exist. How then can we know anything at all about them?

2. Given a "possible worlds" semantics for counterfactual conditionals, it is hard to see why most people do not consider them all to be false. A counterfactual conditional is supposed to be an *existential* claim about worlds beyond this one—a claim that *there is* a world of a certain kind which is more like our world than any other world of some kind. But most people do not think that there are any such worlds. They do not believe in the make-believe worlds of their childhood or in the fantasy worlds of C.S. Lewis. Ask them, and they will say that such worlds do not exist. David Lewis thinks that these worlds exist, although not in, or as part of, the actual world.[4] But his views are unusual. Therefore, to explain why most people do not consider all counterfactual conditionals to be false, it must be supposed that they do not understand what they are saying when they assert them. For, if they thought that in asserting a counterfactual conditional they would be making a claim about the existence worlds beyond this one, they would not wish to assert it.

3. Since other possible worlds are causally isolated from us, it is not clear what difference it would make to us whether what we thought about them was true or false. Hence, anyone who accepts a "possible worlds" semantics for counterfactuals owes us some explanation of why we should have rational systems of beliefs concerning them. The classical answer to the question "Why be rational?" is "Only if one is rational could all of one's beliefs be true." And this answer is considered to be satisfactory, because having true beliefs about what exists in the actual world presumably has some relevance to human interests. But what human interests would be served by having true beliefs about the existence of worlds with which we cannot in any way interact, and which we know not to be actual?[5] If none of our interests is served, then what does it matter whether we accept or reject any counterfactual conditional? Why should we not just consider them all to be true, and stick to the material conditional?

4. I think that Davidson is right in saying that a satisfactory truth theory for a language should help to explain how the language is learnable.[6] If 'α' is any sentence of a language L, then the truth theory for L,

'α' is true iff α,

while formally satisfactory, is trivial. What is required is a specification of truth conditions for the sentences L which is recursive, and proceeds from a finite base of sentences or predicates whose satisfaction conditions can be assumed to be understood. But "possible worlds" semantics for counterfactual conditionals do not proceed from such a base. For, since we have no independent access to other possible worlds, we could have no knowledge of them which was not based upon hypothetical reasoning about them, and hence dependent upon our knowledge of counterfactuals. I think that Goodman has convincingly demonstrated this.[7] Therefore, a "possible worlds" semantics for counterfactual conditionals does not help to explain how we understand them—although it may help us to explain how we understand complex sentences involving them.

5. There are undoubtedly very close semantic links between conditionals in the various tenses and moods. Which grammatical form it is appropriate to use in order to express given belief seems to depend only on the time and circumstances of utterance, and on the background knowledge which the utterer possesses. Let O be a given occasion. Then the two conditionals

> (1) If A *happens* on occasion O, then C will happen on this occasion.
> (2) If A *happened* on occasion O, then C would have happened on this occasion.

are sentences which can be used to say the same thing. And when so used, anything which would be grounds for accepting or rejecting (1) would, if known at the time, be grounds for accepting or rejecting (2). The difference between (1) and (2) is thus a difference only of assertability conditions.[8] (1) is assertable only if one thinks O to be a present or future occasion, and (2) is assertable only if one thinks O to be a past occasion. (2) is just a past tense version of (1). If (1) is uttered before the occasion O, and (2) afterwards, then (1) and (2) say the same thing in the sense in which "It will rain today" said here, today, says the same as "It rained yesterday" said here, tomorrow. But now consider:

> (3) If A *had happened* on occasion O, then C would have happened on this occasion.

The sentences (2) and (3) can likewise be used to say the same thing. And they too differ from each other only in assertability conditions. (3) is properly assertable only if one thinks that A did not happen, and (2) is properly assertable only if one thinks that A might, for all one knows, have happened.

The indicative conditional (1), and the corresponding subjunctive conditional (3), are therefore, very closely related semantically, and any adequate theory of conditionals should be able to account for this fact. But on the most commonly held view, "possible worlds" semantics are required *only* for the analysis of *subjunctive conditionals*, like (3). Ordinary indicative conditionals, like (1), are considered to be material ones. On this view, at least, the close semantic link between indicatives and their corresponding subjunctives cannot be explained.

6. My final objection[9] to "possible worlds" semantics for counterfactuals is an objection also to the theory of conditionals which I shall develop below. The objection runs:

(1) There is a thesis T1 which every adequate logic of counterfactuals must contain
(2) There is a thesis T2 which no adequate logic of counterfactuals can contain
(3) On any standard "possible worlds" semantics in which T1 holds, T2 also holds.

The relevant theses are:

T1. $((\alpha\vee\beta)\square\!\!\rightarrow\!\psi)\supset(\alpha\square\!\!\rightarrow\!\psi)$
T2. $(\alpha\square\!\!\rightarrow\!\psi)\supset((\alpha\wedge\beta)\square\!\!\rightarrow\!\psi)$

The proof is:

(a) Suppose that A and B are logically equivalent. Then every A-world is a B-world and conversely. Therefore, any objective relationships which may hold between A-worlds and other worlds also holds between B-worlds and these other worlds. Therefore if "$A\square\!\!\rightarrow\!C$" is true at world i so is "$B\square\!\!\rightarrow\!C$."

(b) Suppose that T1 is a thesis and that "$\alpha\square\!\!\rightarrow\!\psi$" is true at world i. Then "$((\alpha\wedge\beta)\vee(\alpha\wedge\sim\beta))\square\!\!\rightarrow\!\psi$" is true at world i, and hence by T1, "$(\alpha\wedge\beta)\square\!\!\rightarrow\!\psi$" is true at world i. Therefore T2 is also a thesis.

Therefore, no adequate "possible worlds" semantics of the standard kind is possible for a language which includes counterfactual conditionals.

The argument rests on the assumption that T1 should be a thesis of any adequate logic of counterfactuals; and this may be doubted. But I know of no clear counterexamples to this thesis. Moreover, if simplification of disjunctive antecedents (as T1 is called) is not a thesis, then in the corresponding quantificational theory

$$T3 \quad ((\exists xFx)\square{\rightarrow}\beta) \supset \forall x(Fx\square{\rightarrow}\beta),$$

(where x does not occur free in β), should not be a thesis. But T3 is also very plausible. "If anyone had seen the accident, then the culprit would have been caught" does seem to imply that "Everyone is such that if he had seen the accident then the culprit would have been caught", and in particular, "If John had seen the accident, then the culprit would have been caught." T3, like T1 seems to be undeniable, but it is difficult to see how one could have T3 on any "possible worlds" semantics without also having T1, or conversely.

These six objections are presented only as difficulties for any seriously intended "possible worlds" semantics for counterfactual conditionals. I take the Kuhnian point that to refute a good theory we require a better one. And Lewis' theory, upon which I have chosen to hang my objections, is an elegant and powerful theory which explains most of our intuitions about the validity or otherwise of arguments involving counterfactuals. These objections do, however, provide some points for comparison between Lewis' and other "possible worlds" theories and mine. The first two objections are specific to "possible worlds" semantics for counterfactuals. There are no equivalent or parallel objections to the theory to be developed below. The third objection, concerning the *justification* for being rational about counterfactual conditionals, is not a serious problem for the theory of rational belief systems, since I do not suppose that we have any choice in the matter. It is, however, a problem to explain why human beings think and reason hypothetically as they do.

The fourth objection, about the learnability of the language, is, I think, better dealt with on the theory of rational belief systems. It is true that what conditionals may be accepted as true or false in a rational belief system depends at least in part on what other conditionals are accepted. So my theory has this much in common with "possible worlds" semantics. But I can explain how we may come to understand counterfactual conditionals, once we have understood ordinary present tense indicative ones. We come to understand them by processes similar to those by which we come to understand statements about the past. Given that

(1) If *A happens* on occasion *O*, then *C* will happen on this occasion,

is understood, it is not hard to see how

(3) If *A had happened* on occasion *O*, then *C* would have happened on this occasion

comes to be understood. And, again the theory of conditionals which I shall develop, the processes by which we acquire an understanding of such present tense indicative conditionals as (1) are simple enough to understand.

The fifth objection, therefore, does not apply to my theory of conditionals. The sixth objection, however, is a serious one for both kinds of theories. It is the case to which I referred when I spoke of there being, apparently, a serious discrepancy between the structural features of ordinary human belief systems, and the theoretical structural features of ideally rational ones.[10] In section 4 of this chapter I will argue that an "or" occurring as the principal sentential connective in the antecedent of a conditional (so that the antecedent appears to have the form "$\alpha \lor \beta$") is not a disjunction, but a wide-scope conjunction. Confirmation of this hypothesis is to be found in Japanese where a similar distinction is made. This hypothesis is also available to defenders of "possible worlds" semantics, and indeed, it was suggested to me by David Lewis himself—although, as far as I know, he was not aware of any independent confirmation for it. The sixth objection, therefore, is neutral between Lewis' semantics and mine, and can be met by an auxiliary hypothesis which has independent support.

2. Languages with Conditionals

A conditional language has the syntactic structure of the modal sentential calculus, but has an additional sentential connective, '$\rightarrow$'. For any such language LV, we specify that a rational belief system B on LV satisfies the requirements C1 to C9, and

C13   (a) $T(\alpha \rightarrow \beta)$ occurs in B only if there is no member of $E(B'_\alpha)$ in which $F\beta$ occurs

     (b) $F(\alpha \rightarrow \beta)$ occurs in B only if there is some member of $E(B'_\alpha)$ in which $F\beta$ occurs.

C14   (a) $E(B) \subset E(B'_\alpha)$ if $T\alpha \in B$

    (b) A member of $E(B'_\alpha)$ in which $T\beta$ occurs is a member of $E(B'_{\alpha\wedge\beta})$

    (c) If some member of $E(B'_{\alpha\wedge\beta})$ is a member of $E(B'_\alpha)$, then every member of $E(B'_{\alpha\wedge\beta})$ is a member of $E(B'_\alpha)$

    (d) If $B'_{\alpha\wedge\beta}$ is a rational belief system on LV, then so are B'_α and B'_β

where $E(B'_\alpha)$ is the set of all completed extensions of B'_α, and B'_α is a belief system which is defined in relation to B, and in which $T\alpha$ occurs. The various conditional languages differ from each other only in how B'_α is defined relative to B.

In these requirements, B'_α may be thought of as *the basis* from which one would reason on the supposition that α. Hence, $E(B'_\alpha)$ will be the set of all completed extensions of a belief system B'_α which contains just those beliefs which would be retained, or additionally assumed, if one were reasoning hypothetically from this supposition. The requirement C13(a) then simply states that in any rational belief system, the conditional "$\alpha \rightarrow \beta$" is accepted as true only if $F\beta$ does not occur in any rational extension of this basis.

The requirement, C14(a) is equivalent to the claim that B must be an extension of B'_α if $T\alpha$ occurs in B. That is, if 'α' is already accepted as true, then the basis from which one should reason from the supposition that α should be compatible with what one already believes, and contain no additional suppositions. The only objection which is likely to be made to this requirement is that it is too weak. For, it is plausible to suppose that where 'α' is already accepted as true, then one's basis for reasoning from this supposition should include *everything* that one believes—whether or not it is relevant to the supposition. The requirement C14(a) might therefore be replaced by an equivalent of Lewis' *strong centering requirement*:[11]

C14   (e) $B'_\alpha = B$, if $T\alpha \in B$.

The trouble with C14(e) is that it forces us to count such sentences as "If the weather is fine today, then I had bacon and eggs for breakfast yesterday" as true, if both antecedent and consequent are accepted as true, which is, perhaps, counterintuitive. However, since conditionals with such epistemically and theoretically unrelated antecedents and consequents are rarely asserted or denied, there is no established practice of accepting or rejecting them to which we can appeal to settle the matter, and the choice between C14(a) and C14(e) must be made on other grounds.

The requirements C14(b) and (c) both follow from a single general principle. The principle is that if $T\beta$ occurs in any rational extension B^* of B'_α, then $B'_{\alpha \wedge \beta}$ is a rational extension of B'_α which is compatible with B^*. By a *rational extension* of a belief system I mean any extension of it which is itself a rational belief system. To say that two belief systems are *compatible* is just to say that they have a common rational extension. The general principle can be split naturally into two parts:

(1) If $T\beta$ occurs in any rational extension of B'_α then $B'_{\alpha \wedge \beta}$ is a rational extension of B'_α.

(2) If $T\beta$ occurs in any rational extension B^* of B'_α then B^* is compatible with $B'_{\alpha \wedge \beta}$.

The first part, (1), is that if $T\beta$ is compatible with B'_α, then the basis from which one would reason from the joint supposition that both α and β should include the basis for reasoning from just the supposition that α. That is, if it can be done consistently, the basis for reasoning from this joint supposition may be constructed by first making the supposition that α and then the *further supposition* that β. If 'α' and 'β' are any two quite unrelated suppositions, such as, that it is fine today, and that I had bacon and eggs for breakfast yesterday, it would be strange indeed if my basis for reasoning from the joint supposition was not a simple rational extension of my basis for reasoning from either supposition alone. Now, if some member of $E(B'_{\alpha \wedge \beta})$ is a member of $E(B'_\alpha)$, then $T\beta$ occurs in some rational extension of B'_α, and therefore, $B'_{\alpha \wedge \beta}$ is a rational extension of B'_α, and therefore, every member of $E(B'_{\alpha \wedge \beta})$ is a member of $E(B'_\alpha)$. Hence the requirement C14(c).

The second part, (2), of the principle is that any rational extension of B'_α in which $T\beta$ occurs should be compatible with $B'_{\alpha \wedge \beta}$. That is, if $T\beta$ is compatible with B'_α, then one can consider what must occur in rational extensions of $B'_{\alpha \wedge \beta}$ just by limiting attention to rational extensions of B'_α in which $T\beta$ occurs. That is, given the compatibility of $T\beta$ with one's basis for reasoning from the supposition that α, there cannot be any rational extensions of this basis which are compatible with $T\beta$ but incompatible with $B'_{\alpha \wedge \beta}$. If this were not so, then $B'_{\alpha \wedge \beta}$ would be a gratuitously strong basis for reasoning from the joint supposition. And I cannot see that there could be any rational justification for assuming such a basis. Now, if any rational extension B^* of B'_α in which $T\beta$ occurs must be compatible with $B'_{\alpha \wedge \beta}$, then every completed extension of B^* must be a completed extension of $B'_{\alpha \wedge \beta}$. Therefore, any member of $E(B'_\alpha)$

in which $T\beta$ occurs must be a member of $E(B'_{\alpha \wedge \beta})$. Hence the requirement, C14(b).

The last requirement, C14(d), on bases of hypothetical reasoning, is an obvious one. It is just that if one's basis for reasoning from the joint supposition that both α and β is rational, then one's basis for reasoning from either conjunct alone must be rational. If the bases from which anyone reasoned hypothetically appeared to violate any of these requirements, then I think we should require an explanation of why this was so.

For any belief system B on a conditional language LV let $B + T\alpha$ be a belief system which differs from B only by inclusion of $T\alpha$ in place of $X\alpha$ if $X\alpha$ occurs in B, or by inclusion of $T\alpha$ in addition to $F\alpha$ if $F\alpha$ occurs in B, or *does not differ from B if $T\alpha$ occurs in B*. Then, compatibly with the requirements, C14, B'_α may be variously defined. I consider four possible definitions of B'_α.

D1. $\quad B'_\alpha =_{df} B + T\alpha$

_____

For B'_α defined in this way,

$$(\alpha \to \beta) \equiv (\alpha \supset \beta)$$

is a tautology of LV. Hence we may replace the arrow as defined in C13 and D1 by '$\supset$', the *material conditional*.

D2. $\quad B'_\alpha =_{df} B' + T\alpha$

_____

where B' is defined as for some modal language. For B'_α defined in this way,

$$(\alpha \to \beta) \equiv \Box(\alpha \supset \beta)$$

is a tautology of LV. Hence, we may replace the arrow as defined in D2 and C13, by '$\dashrightarrow$', the *strict conditional*. What kind of strict conditional it is depends on how B' is defined in relation to B.

D3. $\quad B'_\alpha =_{df} B^*_\alpha + T\alpha$

_____

where B^*_α is a belief system on LV such that
(a) $T\beta \in B^*_\alpha$ if $T\Box\beta$ or $T(\alpha \to \beta)$ occurs in B
(b) B^*_α is otherwise agnostic

For B'_α defined in this way, the conditional arrow is the *variably strict*, "$\Box\!\!\to$", of Lewis' systems, and the resulting logic of conditionals is his system VW. To obtain Lewis' preferred system VC, the strong centering requirement, C14(e), must be included among the requirements on bases of hypothetical reasoning.

D4. $B'_\alpha =_{df} B^+_\alpha + T\alpha$

where B^+_α is a belief system on LV such that

(a) $T\beta \in B^+_\alpha$ if $T\Box\beta$ or $T(\alpha\to\beta)$ occurs in B.
(b) $F\beta \in B^+_\alpha$ if $F(\alpha\to\beta)$ occurs in B.
(c) B^+_α is otherwise agnostic.

If C14(e) is included among the requirements on the bases of hypothetical reasoning, and B'_α is defined as on D4, then the resulting logic of conditionals is Stalnaker's system VCS.

Let us call the language in which B'_α is defined as in D3 and for which the bases of hypothetical reasoning satisfy the requirements C14(a) to (d), the language LVW, and that for which the bases of hypothetical reasoning satisfy C14(b) to (e), the language LVC. Let LVCS be the Stalnaker language defined *via* D4 and the requirements C14(b) to (e). Then, the tautologies of LVW, LVC and LVCS are the theorems of VW, VC and VCS respectively.

The general theory of conditionals here developed is a *suppositional theory*. A conditional "$\alpha\to\beta$" should be accepted as true in any completed extension of one's belief system B, if 'β' would be so accepted in every completed extension of a belief system B'_α which is a function of B, and includes the supposition that α. The kind of conditional involved depends upon how B'_α is defined in relation to B. If $B'_\alpha =_{df} B + T\alpha$, then the conditional is a material conditional. That is, if in addition to the supposition that α, B'_α must include *everything* that one would claim to know, and continue to do so as more information is obtained, then $T(\alpha\to\beta)$ will occur in a rational completion of one's belief system iff $T(\alpha\supset\beta)$ also occurs. For those who think that ordinary indicative conditionals are material conditionals, the definition D1 should be acceptable. If $B'_\alpha =_{df} B' + T\alpha$, where B' includes just those of one's beliefs which one would take to be in some fixed sense, *necessarily true*, then the conditional is strict. There appears to be no special locution in English for expressing strict conditionals; so, perhaps this is not a very interesting case. But if, for formal purposes, anyone wished to have a strict conditional in the language, D2 would provide an elegant way of defining it. If $B'_\alpha =_{df} B^*_\alpha + T\alpha$, where B^*_α includes not only what we would take to be necessarily true, but also what we think would still be or have been the case if 'α' were, then the conditional is variably strict. At least some conditionals of English appear to be of this kind, and the theory provides a simple way of defining them.

For those who are devoted to "possible worlds" semantics, a possible world may be thought of as a world truly described by some completed belief system. Accordingly, $E(B'_\alpha)$ will be a set of descriptions of possible worlds in which 'α' is true. But $E(B'_\alpha)$ may not contain descriptions of all possible α-worlds, because some member of $E(B'_{\alpha \wedge \beta})$ may exist even though $F\beta$ occurs in every member of $E(B'_\alpha)$. If this is the case, then on Lewis' picture of the way things are, the nearest $(\alpha \wedge \beta)$-worlds must be more remote from the actual world than the nearest α-worlds. Informally, $E(B'_\alpha)$ may be thought of as the set of *nearest* α-worlds and $E(B)$ as the set of worlds which, for all we know, might be actual. The requirements C14 may then be read:

(a) If the actual world is known to be an α-world, then the set of worlds which, for all we know, might be actual is a subset of the set of nearest α-worlds.

(b) A member of the set of nearest α-worlds which is a β-world is a member of the set of nearest $(\alpha \wedge \beta)$-worlds.

(c) If some member of the set of nearest $(\alpha \wedge \beta)$-worlds is a member of the set of nearest α-worlds, then the former is a subset of the latter.

(d) If the set of nearest $(\alpha \wedge \beta)$-worlds is not empty then neither is the set of nearest α-worlds nor the set of nearest β-worlds.

However, I see no reason to take such "possible worlds" semantics seriously. For I see no reason to think that a false but consistent set of beliefs about this world is a true system of beliefs about some other world. A foundation for a logic of conditionals can be provided without this assumption.

Given the requirements on rational belief systems on LVW it is easy to demonstrate that if 'α' is a theorem of VW then 'α' is a tautology of LVW.[12] To prove completeness it is sufficient to note that if a completed belief system B on L is construed as a true description of a possible world W, and the set $E(B'_\alpha)$ as describing the set W_α of α-worlds nearest to W, then for completed belief systems, the requirements C13 and C14 correspond to the *standard* requirements on possible worlds models for VW. C13 corresponds to:

"$\alpha \rightarrow \beta$" is true at W iff 'β' is true at every member of W_α,

C14(a) is Lewis' weak centering requirement, C14(b) corresponds to:

If any member of W_α is a β-world, then it is a member of $W_{\alpha \wedge \beta}$.

C14(c) corresponds to:

If some member of $W_{\alpha \wedge \beta}$ is a member of W_α then every member of $W_{\alpha \wedge \beta}$ is a member of W_α.

And C14(d) is just that if there is any member of $W_{\alpha \wedge \beta}$ then there are also members of W_α and W_β. There cannot, therefore, be any tautologies of LVW which are not theorems of VW.

3. Indicative and Subjunctive Conditionals

It is initially plausible to identify indicative conditionals with material conditionals, and subjunctives with variably strict conditionals. However, I think that in general this would be a mistake. There are good reasons for thinking that an indicative is not normally a material conditional, but that indicative and subjunctive conditionals are usually variant locutions for the one kind of conditional, the logic for which is a logic of variably strict conditionals.

My main reasons for thinking that indicatives are not usually material conditionals are:

1. If an indicative conditional is a material conditional, then the two indicative conditionals "If α then β" and "If not-α then β" cannot both be judged to be false, or improbable. that they cannot both be false is well known. That they cannot both be improbable is a theorem of the probability calculus. It will not do to argue that improbability claims concerning conditionals are really of the form: "$\alpha \supset (P(\beta) < \frac{1}{2})$", because this would imply that conditionals with true antecedents and the same consequent could not differ in probability.[13] Therefore, within the context of a probability claim there is no satisfactory way of representing an indicative conditional as a material conditional.[14]

This argument from the probabilistic paradoxes of material conditionals is stronger than the argument from the ordinary paradoxes for two reasons. First, it cannot be argued that these paradoxes depend on confusions between truth and assertability conditions, because the conditionals said to be improbable may be ordinary indicative conditionals, the antecedents and consequents of which have unknown truth values. Second, it cannot be argued that we have to make do with the material conditional, because we have no better way of representing conditionals within probabilistic contexts. For, provided that the probability of a conditional is independent of the probability of its antecedent, which is surely the normal case, it behaves, logically, like a conditional probability claim,[15] and no such paradoxes arise if probability claims on conditionals are represented in this way. From "$P(\gamma/\alpha)<\frac{1}{2}$" and "$P(\gamma/\sim\alpha)<\frac{1}{2}$" we can deduce "$P(\gamma)<\frac{1}{2}$", which is surely correct. And from "$P(\gamma/\alpha)<\frac{1}{2}$" and "$P(\gamma/\beta)>\frac{1}{2}$", we cannot deduce "$\sim\alpha\lor\sim\beta$", or even $P(\alpha\land\beta)=0$, which again is surely as it should be.

Lewis has argued conclusively that probabilities of conditionals cannot, in general, be conditional probabilities.[16] Nevertheless, for the Stalnaker conditional '$>$', where the probability of a conditional is obtained by *imaging* rather than conditionalization, the following axioms are satisfied, if $Pa \neq 0$.

(1) $P(\alpha>\beta)\leq 1$
(2) $P(\alpha>\beta)+P(\alpha>\sim\beta)=1$
(3) $P(\alpha>(\beta\lor\gamma))=P(\alpha>\beta)+P(\alpha>\beta)-P(\alpha>(\beta\land\gamma))$
(4) $P(\alpha>(\beta\lor\sim\beta))=1$

Moreover, since "$(\alpha\land\beta)\equiv(\alpha\land(\alpha>\beta))$" is a theorem of VCS,

(5) $P(\alpha\land\beta)=P(\alpha\land(\alpha>\beta))$

Therefore, if $P\alpha$ is independent of $P(\alpha>\beta)$, we must also have

(6) $P(\alpha\land\beta)=P\alpha\times P(\alpha>\beta)$

Therefore, the probability of a Stalnaker conditional is the corresponding conditional probability *provided that its probability is independent of the probability of its antecedent*. What Lewis has shown is that for languages in which iterated and nested conditionals may occur this independence condition cannot in general be satisfied.[17]

2. Those who defend the claim that indicative conditionals are material conditionals usually do so on the basis of a distinction between truth and assertability conditions. They claim that it is a violation of assertability conditions to claim that if α then β, if one already knows that 'α' is false or that 'β' is true. They argue that the paradoxes of material implication all derive from violations of such assertability conditions, and hence that arguments based on

such paradoxes do nothing to show that the *truth conditions* for indicative conditionals are not those of material conditionals. The argument would be more convincing if there were any reason to suppose that in any ordinary case the falsity of the antecedent or the truth of the consequent of a conditional ever provided any grounds at all for *accepting* it. If someone asserts a conditional without knowledge of the truth or falsity of either its antecedent or consequent (and so does not violate any assertability conditions) and then later discovers that its antecedent is false or its consequent true, it would be very odd indeed if he were to turn and say "There you see, I was right".

The parallel is often drawn with disjunction. It is said to be a violation of assertability conditions to claim that "α or β" is true, if one already knows that α or knows that β. Nevertheless, the truth of 'α' is a sufficient condition for the truth of "α or β". If someone claims, without violation of assertability conditions, that either Perhaps or How Now will win the Melbourne Cup, then his judgement *is* vindicated if either horse wins. A sufficient ground for accepting a disjunct is a sufficient ground for *accepting* the disjunction, although, once this additional information has been acquired, and the winner declared, it would be misleading to *assert* that either Perhaps or How Now won. But the alleged parallel with conditionals does not hold. For the judgement, made without violation of assertability conditions, that if John goes to the reception he will meet the Ambassador *is not* vindicated by the later discovery that John did not go to the reception. Nor is it vindicated by the discovery that he met the Ambassador the next day in the pub.

3. There are paradoxes generated by construing indicative conditionals as material conditionals which do not in any way depend upon violations of assertability conditions.[18] Consider the following three claims

(a) If John lives in Melbourne, then he lives in Victoria.
(b) If John lives in Sydney, then he lives in Victoria.
(c) If John lives in Melbourne, then he lives in New South Wales.

A rational man can surely consider (a) to be true, and (b) and (c) false. But if the conditionals are material conditionals, then his belief system is inconsistent.

My argument for thinking that indicative and subjunctive

conditionals are normally variant locutions for the one kind of conditional is:

1. An indicative conditional is usually a *conditional prediction*. It is a claim of the form:

(a) If *X occurs* on occasion *O*, then *Y* will occur on this occasion.

If both *X* and *Y* are found to occur, then this conditional prediction is confirmed. If it is found that *X* occurs, but *Y* does not occur, then it is disconfirmed. But if *X* is found not to occur, then this has no bearing on the acceptability or otherwise of the conditional prediction. It may continue to be accepted as true, or it may be rejected in the light of some new information.

2. The indicative conditional

(b) If *X occurred* on occasion *O*, then *Y* (would have) occurred on this occasion

is a *past tense* version of (a). That is, it expresses the same belief as the belief expressed by (a), but does so against the background knowledge that the occasion *O* is now in the past. We may say that (b) expresses the same conditional prediction as (a), but does so *retrospectively*. The conditional prediction expressed is the same in the sense that any epistemic justification for accepting or rejecting the one would, if known at the time, be an epistemic justification for accepting or rejecting the other. What (a) says in prospect about the occasion *O* is just what (b) says in retrospect about this occasion. Therefore, if the implications of the tenses are not relevant to any argument in which (a) or (b) may occur, then these two sentences may be regarded as logically equivalent. A rational man who accepts (or rejects) (a) before the occasion *O*, and rejects (or accepts) (b) afterwards *can only have changed his mind*. He no longer thinks that what he thought before is true.

3. Any two conditionals of the form:
(b) If *X occurred* on occasion *O*, then *Y* (would have) occurred on this occasion
(c) If *X had occurred* on occasion *O*, then *Y* would have occurred on this occasion

are also closely related. The first is a conditional prediction made retrospectively. The second contains the same conditional prediction, but it is made retrospectively against the background knowledge X did not occur. The locution (c) is chosen instead of (b) to indicate this difference of background information. But the conditional prediction which occurs in (c) is still the same as that which occurs in (a) or (b). What (c) says in retrospect, *and in the belief that X did not occur*, in what (b) says in retrospect and (a) says in prospect. Therefore, if the implication of the change of mood from (b) to (c) is not relevant to any argument in which (b) or (c) may occur, then (b) and (c) may be considered to be logically equivalent. A rational man who accepts (or rejects) (b) in the absence of any knowledge of whether X occurred who does not accept (or reject) (c) when he is informed that X did not occur can only have changed his mind. He no longer thinks that what he thought before is true.

4. There is, therefore, a very close epistemic relationship between the indicative conditionals, (a) and (b), and the subjunctive conditional, (c). The only differences between them appear to be in the backgrounds of knowledge or belief against which they are assertable. Hence, these differences might be said to be only ones of assertability conditions. However, the distinction between acceptability and assertability conditions is not a very clear one, and it might be made in various ways, depending on the purposes at hand. Here it is sufficient to point out that the changes of tense and mood in the transition from (a) through (b) to (c) are forced upon us by changes in time and circumstances. Once the events in question have occurred, the locution (b) or (c) is required to express the belief originally expressed in (a). Which particular locution is required depends on what we know about what actually happened on the given occasion. Therefore, in a common and intuitive sense of "saying the same", (a), (b) and (c) all say the same thing. If, before the occasion O, John asserts that if X occurs then Y will occur, then from a later vantage point, in which it is known that X did not occur, it would be correct and fair to report John as having asserted that if X had occurred, Y would have occurred. For certainly, John himself would accept this subjunctive conditional after the event, once he had learned that X did not occur, iff he would still consider his original claim to be true.

5. If the above analysis of the relationship between (a) and (c) is correct, then (a) and (c) may be regarded as different ways of expressing the same belief. They differ from each other in tense and mood, and hence in the circumstances in which it would be

appropriate to assert them. But they contain the same antecedent supposition and the same consequent, and the same considerations are relevant to the acceptability or otherwise of the belief they both express. Let 'α' be the antecedent supposition, 'β' the common consequent, and '$\rightarrow$' conditional connective. Then (a) and (c) both express the belief $T(\alpha \rightarrow \beta)$.

In this case, B'_α, the basis from which one would reason hypothetically from the supposition that α, will include, beside $T\alpha$, any beliefs one would retain or additionally suppose about the events or circumstances *preceding O* when attempting to accommodate this supposition—preceding O, because (a) is a conditional *prediction*. At the time when it would be appropriate to assert (a), B'_α might *contingently* be equal to $B + T\alpha$. If it is not, then some other locution such as

(d) If X were to occur, then Y would occur

might be required. But normally, a conditional prediction is made on a supposition which can simply be added to one's store of beliefs, and for such a prediction a form of expression like (a) is normally appropriate. It should be noted, however, that the *contingent identity* of B'_α and $B + T\alpha$ does not imply that (a) is a material conditional. For it to be a material conditional B'_α would have to remain equal to $B + T\alpha$ however one's belief system B might be expanded.

6. The fact that B'_α and $B + T\alpha$ are often contingently identical, when it is appropriate to assert an indicative conditional like (a), is nevertheless important. For, it helps to explain how hypothetical reasoning is learnable. A child first learns to make and understand conditional predictions in cases where the suppositions involved are compatible with his beliefs. The conditional predictions he accepts are beliefs of some kind—beliefs which may be confirmed or disconfirmed by later discoveries. These beliefs normally refer to particular occasions. When these occasions have passed, the beliefs may remain. And, if in a particular case, he finds that the supposition on which he has made a conditional prediction is not realized, then he learns that in order to express his belief he must use a subjunctive conditional. In principle, this is like learning to make statements about the past, and the processes involved are no more difficult. There is, therefore, no great mystery about how we learn to use and understand subjunctive conditionals. We under-

stand them because we understand the simple indicative conditionals for which they are, essentially, variant locutions.

7. The above theory of the relationship between indicative and subjunctive conditionals explains why it is so important, in assessing the truth or falsity of a subjunctive, to consider mainly the events or circumstances which occurred or existed *before* the occasion on which the antecedent is supposed to have been realized. For, these are the events and circumstances which are most relevant to assessing the truth or falsity of the corresponding indicative, which we may imagine to have been asserted before the relevant occasion, and in the absence of any knowledge that its antecedent would not be fulfilled. If we have very good evidence that Y would occur if X occurs in circumstances relevantly similar to those which existed then, then we may pronounce the counterfactual "If X had occurred, then Y would have occurred" to be true. And this claim will be defensible, even if a world in which both X and Y occurred would be very much less like the actual world than any in which X occurred but Y still did not occur.

The two recent papers, Lewis and Jackson stress the importance of *antecedent similarity* in the comparison of worlds.[19] According to Jackson, a sequential counterfactual "$\alpha\square\rightarrow\beta$" is true at the actual world iff there is a possible world governed by the same causal laws as ours in which both 'α' and 'β' are true and which is *antecedently* more similar to the actual world than any such world in which 'α' is true and 'β' false. The theory of conditionals here presented explains and justifies this emphasis.

8. Given that a subjunctive conditional expresses a conditional prediction retrospectively against the background information that its antecedent has not been fulfilled, and hence that the belief which it expresses is a belief which, at another time, and in other circumstances, might have been expressed by an indicative conditional, the laws governing the structure of rational belief systems on languages in which such subjunctive conditionals occur must be the same as those which govern the structure of rational belief systems on languages in which indicative conditionals occur. That is, the logic of indicatives must be the same as the logic of subjunctive conditionals. Those who think that indicative conditionals are material conditionals might wish to use this as an argument that subjunctive conditionals are also material conditionals. However, as we have already seen, there are good reasons for thinking that indicative conditionals are not, ordinarily,

material ones. And the arguments for thinking that subjunctive conditionals are not material conditionals are overwhelming. Hence, the common logic of all ordinary conditionals, whether indicative or subjunctive, must be a logic applicable to subjunctive conditionals, such as Lewis' VW or VC. With perhaps some rare exceptions, all conditionals should be considered to be variably strict.

9. If indicative conditionals are normally variably strict, then it is not hard to explain the phenomena which have proved recalcitrant on the theory of indicatives as material conditionals. For there is no reason why "$\alpha\square\rightarrow\beta$" and "$\sim\alpha\square\rightarrow\beta$" should not both be considered to be false or improbable. There is no reason to suppose that either the discovery that "α" is false, or that 'β' is true vindicates the judgement that "$\alpha\square\rightarrow\beta$" is true. And there is no reason why a rational man should not consider it to be true that if John lives in Melbourne, then he lives in Victoria, but deny that if he lives in Melbourne then he lives in New South Wales, and also deny that if he lives in Sydney, then he lives in Victoria.

The theory of subjunctive conditionals here presented meets most of the main objections to "possible worlds" theories. Firstly, the theory does not require us to believe in, or claim to know anything at all about, other possible worlds. If such things exist, we shall never know about them. Secondly, the theory explains how knowledge of counterfactuals is possible, and how we may come to understand them. On the theory presented, there is no great difficulty in seeing how a language in which counterfactual conditionals occur is learnable. On "possible worlds" theories this remains a mystery. The theory explains the close epistemic relationship between subjunctive conditionals and corresponding indicatives. On theories in which subjunctives and indicative conditionals express radically different kinds of claims, this is unexplained. The theory also explains the supreme importance of antecedent similarity in the comparison of possible worlds. On "possible worlds" theories the adoption of the antecedent similarity criterion is *ad hoc.*

There are, however, some difficulties which should be considered. and two which require extensive treatment. The two requiring extensive treatment are:

(1) The problem of simplification of disjunctive antecedents already mentioned in Section 2, and

(2) The problem of the relationship between probability claims

on conditionals and conditional probability claims. What is at issue, here, is whether these can be identified. For, it seems to be required by the logical correspondence principle and the argument relating to the probabilistic paradoxes of material conditionals, that they should be the same.

These two problems will be dealt with in the following sections. Here, we shall be concerned only with a specific counterexample[20] to the main thesis of this section, viz., that indicative and subjunctive conditionals are normally variant locutions for the one general kind of conditional. The indicative conditional:

(a) If Oswald did not kill Kennedy, then someone else did,

is not related epistemically to:

(b) If Oswald had not killed Kennedy, then someone else would have, in the way that the theory requires.

For a rational man may accept (a) and simultaneously reject (b). Therefore, not every subjunctive conditional corresponds to an indicative in the way required by the theory.

It is clear that (a) and (b) make quite different claims, i.e., that they are not alternative ways of saying the same thing. The statement (b) corresponds not to (a), but to

(c) If Oswald *does* not kill Kennedy, then someone else *will.*

The statement (c) says in prospect what (b) says in retrospect against the (supposed) background knowledge that Oswald killed Kennedy. The difficulty, therefore, is not with (b), for which there is a corresponding indicative, but with (a) which looks like, but is not, a past tense version of (c). Therefore, the argument does not show that there are subjunctives which do not correspond to indicatives in the way required by the theory, but that there may be indicatives, like (a), for which there are no corresponding subjunctives.

The conditional (a) is arguably a material conditional, since it appears to be epistemically equivalent to (i.e., to have the same acceptability conditions as)

(d) Someone killed Kennedy.

To construe (a) as a variably strict conditional, B'_α must be taken to include knowledge which, together with the supposition that Oswald did not kill Kennedy, implies that someone else killed him. That is, it must be supposed that conditions prior to the assassination were such that if Oswald did not try, or failed in his attempt, then someone else would succeed. But I think that anyone who asserts (a) would not expect to be thus understood to be asserting (c) retrospectively. Rather, he would expect to be understood to be making a *post facto* remark in the light of the knowledge that someone killed Kennedy, and making the obvious point that it was either Oswald or someone else. Therefore, I think that (a) should be considered to be a material conditional. But as such it is an atypical conditional. In an ordinary conditional, whether it is expressed indicatively or subjunctively, there is alleged to be some physical connection between antecedent and consequent conditions or events. In this case there is none.

4. *Simplification of Disjunctive Antecedents*

The problem of simplification of disjunctive antecedents is a major problem both for "possible worlds" theories of counter-factuals and for the theory of conditionals developed in this chapter. The problem is that

(a) If X or Y were to happen then Z would occur

seems to imply

(b) If X were to happen then Z would occur

There are no good counter-examples to this thesis. And yet, if "$((\alpha \vee \beta) \square \rightarrow \gamma) \supset (\alpha \square \rightarrow \gamma)$" is a thesis, then "$(\alpha \square \rightarrow \gamma) \supset ((\alpha \wedge \beta) \square \rightarrow \gamma)$" must also be. The argument for this does not depend on the details of any particular "possible worlds" theories. It applies to any theory in which the truth of a counterfactual depends on relationships between possible worlds in which its antecedent is true and other possible worlds. Since every α-world is an $((\alpha \wedge \beta) \vee (\alpha \wedge \sim \beta))$-world, and conversely, any relationship which holds between an α-world and other possible worlds must also be a relationship which holds between an $((\alpha \wedge \beta) \vee (\alpha \wedge \sim \beta))$-world and these other worlds. Therefore, if "$\alpha \square \rightarrow \beta$" is true in virtue of some such relationship, "$((\alpha \wedge \beta) \vee (\alpha \wedge \sim \beta)) \square \rightarrow \gamma$" must also be true. Therefore, if simplification of disjunctive antecedents is a thesis, and "$\alpha \square \rightarrow \gamma$" is true, then so is "$(\alpha \wedge \beta) \square \rightarrow \gamma$."

But this is not only a problem for possible worlds theories. Any *completed* rational belief system in which $T\alpha$ occurs is one in which $T((\alpha \wedge \beta) \vee (\alpha \wedge \sim \beta))$ also occurs, and conversely. Hence, the supposition that α is surely the same as the supposition that

$((\alpha \wedge \beta) \vee (\alpha \wedge \sim\beta))$. But, if this is so, then $B'_\alpha = B'_{((\alpha \wedge \beta) \vee (\alpha \wedge \sim\beta))}$. Hence if $F\gamma$ does not occur in any member of $E(B'_\alpha)$ then it does not occur in any member of $E(B'_{(\alpha \wedge \beta) \vee (\alpha \wedge \sim\beta)})$, and conversely. Therefore, if $T(\alpha \square \!\!\rightarrow \gamma)$ occurs in any completed rational belief system, $T(((\alpha \wedge \beta) \vee (\alpha \wedge \sim\beta)) \square \!\!\rightarrow \gamma)$ also occurs, and conversely. Therefore, if simplification of disjunctive antecedents is a thesis, and $T(\alpha \square \!\!\rightarrow \gamma)$ occurs in some rational belief system B, then $F((\alpha \wedge \beta) \square \!\!\rightarrow \gamma)$ does not also occur in B.

The only way I know of dealing with this problem is to challenge the assumption that an "or" which occurs in a disjunctive antecedent of a conditional is properly transcribed by '$\vee$'. David Lewis has suggested to me (in conversation) that an "or" occurring in this position functions as a *wide-scope conjunction*. Certainly, "$(\alpha \text{ or } \beta) \square \!\!\rightarrow \psi$" and "$(\alpha \square \!\!\rightarrow \psi)$ *and* $(\beta \square \!\!\rightarrow \psi)$" appear to be logically equivalent in English. But since this is precisely the basis of the objection, it does nothing to show that the antecedent "or" is a wide-scope conjunction. It would be more to the point if it could be shown that an "or" in the antecendent position behaves abnormally in other ways. For example, if "$(\sim(\alpha \text{ or } \beta)) \square \!\!\rightarrow \psi$" were not equivalent to "$(\sim\alpha \text{ and } \sim\beta) \square \!\!\rightarrow \psi$" then we should have some grounds for thinking that the "or" was not an ordinary disjunction.[21] But an "or" in the antecedent position does behave normally under negation; so there is no support here for Lewis' suggestion.

Nevertheless, I am inclined to think that Lewis' suggestion may be right. There is some support for this position in Japanese.[22] The Japanese have several different words for each of "and" and "or", but two of them are of particular interest; because they would sometimes be translated into English by "and" and sometimes by "or", depending on the context. The two connectives are "ya" and "tari". "Ya" is an *incomplete* sort of "and" which one uses when one is naming some, but presumably not all, of the members of some (usually contextually implied) class. Thus, if a Japanese wishes to say that he went to the park *and* to the school, and does not wish to imply that these are the only places he visited, then he will use the conjunction "ya". The word "ya" is a noun conjunction. The word (or rather, verb-ending) "tari" is the corresponding verbal or sentential conjunction. Thus, if I wish to say, in Japanese, that while I was in Sydney I visited the zoo *and* (I) swam at Bondi, but do not wish to imply that these are the only things I did, then I should use the connective "tari" to translate "and."

The noun conjunction "ya" is to be distinguished from the noun conjunctions "mo" and "to." "Mo" is used when one wishes to refer to two or more things which are to be considered together in some way. Thus if I wish to say, in Japanese, that the combination of oysters and clams makes me ill, I do not say that oysters *ya* clams make me ill, for that is to imply that each separately does so, and that they are not the only things of the kind which do so. Rather, I should say that oysters *mo* clams make me ill. The former, but not the latter, implies that oysters make me ill *and* clams make me ill. "To" is a complete conjunction which is used when one is listing exhaustively the things one is speaking about. Thus if a Japanese wishes to say that he went to the shop to buy some bread *and* some milk, and does not wish to imply that these are just some of, or are just typical of, the things he went to buy, then he would use the noun conjunction "to." To use "ya" in this context would be to imply that he went to buy some bread and some milk *and other things like that.* Corresponding to the noun conjunctions "mo" and "to" are the sentential or verbal conjunctions "shi" and "te." These correspond to "mo" and "to", respectively, in roughly the way that "tari" corresponds to "ya."

All of these connectives are to be distinguished from the Japanese disjunction "ka" which may be either a noun, a verbal or a sentential disjunction. "Ka" has the sense of an *exclusive* disjunction, unless the implication of exclusiveness is explicitly cancelled by an additional phrase which means roughly "or both."

What is particularly interesting about the connectives "ya" and "tari" is that they are often used to translate "or." Thus, to translate "I did not go to the beach *or* to the zoo" it would be appropriate to use the word "ya." And these are the words which, typically, are used to translate conditionals with (apparently) disjunctive antecedents. Thus, to translate "If I eat oysters *or* clams then I will become ill", the Japanese will say "If I eat oysters *ya* clams then I will become ill"; and the same applies to the counterfactual "If I had eaten either the oysters or the clams then I would have become ill." Similarly, to translate "If my son is (were to be) expelled from school *or* my daughter drops out (were to drop out) from university, then there will (would) be a row at home" the word "tari" is required to translate "or." One could therefore argue that the word "or", in a "disjunctive" antecedent of a conditional, functions as a kind of incomplete conjunction, indicating that one is listing some, but presumably not all of the conditions under which the consequent would be true.

One could gain some support for Lewis' suggestion by arguing that the distinction between "anything" and "everything" is just a generalization of that between "ya" and "to." "Anything you say may be taken down and used in evidence" does not mean the same as "Everything you say may be taken down and used in evidence." The former entails the latter, but not conversely. For let x range over things said by you, and 'D' and 'E' be the predicates "taken down" and "used in evidence" respectively. Then the first claim is that $\forall x \Diamond (Dx \wedge Ex)$ while the second is that $\Diamond \forall x (Dx \wedge Ex)$. The word "anything" thus functions as a quantifier of wider scope than "everything", since it occurs outside the modality. Likewise "If anyone had seen the accident then the culprit would have been caught" does not mean the same as "If everyone had seen the accident then the culprit would have been caught." The word "anyone" in this context is a wide-scope universal quantifier which lies outside the scope of the conditional connective.

That the word "anyone" in the antecedent of a conditional does *at least sometimes* function as a wide-scope universal quantifier has to be admitted, because there is no other way of explaining how an "anyone" in this position could bind a variable in the consequent clause. For example, in the sentence "If *anyone* had seen the accident then *he* would have been shocked" the word "he" is obviously not a free variable, and there is no way of transcribing the sentence into logical symbolism without using a universal quantifier for "anyone." Only a universal quantifier which lies outside the scope of the conditional connective will do the trick. One could therefore argue that it would be just *ad-hocery* to suppose that the word "anyone" might change its rôle from that of a wide-scope universal quantifier to one of a narrow-scope existential quantifier when it so happens that there is no variable in the consequent clause for it to bind. One could therefore say that T3 is no more acceptable as a thesis than T1. It could be claimed that there are no clear examples of English sentences which have the form "$\exists x\alpha \square \rightarrow \psi$" or any which have the form "$(\alpha \vee \beta) \square \rightarrow \psi$." Every sentence which is apparently of one of these forms contains either a wide-scope conjunction or a wide-scope universal quantifier in its antecedent.

But this way of resolving the difficulty leads to others. For what account can be given of the fact that the negation of an "either ... or ..." antecedent in a subjunctive conditional is an ordinary "neither ... nor ..." antecedent. "If it were not the case that either α or β, then ... " is equivalent to "If it were neither the case that α nor the case that β, then ..." Are we to suppose that a negation operator transforms a wide-scope conjunction into an ordinary disjunction before it takes effect? There is a similar difficulty with wide-scope universal quantifiers. The sentence "If it were not the case that anyone had seen the accident, then the culprit would have been caught" is equivalent to "If no one had seen the accident, then the culprit would have been caught." Does the negation operator, then, transform the wide-scope universal quantifier into a narrow scope existential quantifier before negating it? If so, why? And why has it not been clear all along that a negation in such an antecedent does more than negate the antecedent?

One could reply to the second of these points that it *is* sometimes obvious that negating a wide-scope universal quantifier narrows its scope. If I say "If it were not the case that anyone had seen the accident then he would have been shocked" then I invite the response "Who's he?" Once the negation operator is inserted, the "he" is no longer bound by the quantifier. Its scope has been narrowed by negation. Moreover, since the antecedent clause here is equivalent to "If no one had seen the accident ...", then the original quantifier has not only been narrowed in scope by negation, but transformed in the process into an existential quantifier before being negated. If all of this happens (as apparently it does in this case), then we have to admit that inserting a negation operator before a wide-scope universal quantifier in the antecedent of a conditional radically changes the logical structure of the whole sentence. At least, we have to admit that it does so in this case, so why not in all cases? And if a negation operator can change a wide-scope universal quantifier into a narrow-scope existential quantifier, why should we not suppose that it operates in the same way in the finite case and changes a wide-scope conjunction into a narrow-scope disjunction?

But even if a negation operator does all of these things, the question remains: Why? When someone says:

(a) If A or B had been the case, then C would have been the case

(b) If neither A nor B had been the case, then D would have been the case

one normally thinks of the antecedents of (a) and (b) as being a *pair* of mutually exclusive and jointly exhaustive assumptions. But this can be the case only if the "or" occurring in (a) is an ordinary disjunction. Similarly, the antecedents of

    (c) If anything had been an *F*, then *A* would have been the case
    (d) If nothing had been an *F*, then *B* would have been the case

are thought of as a pair of mutually exclusive and jointly exhaustive assumptions. And again, this can be the case only if the "anything" in (c) is thought of as an existential quantifier. How are we to account for these intuitions? Anyone who accepts both T1 and T3 as theses should have no difficulty in doing so. He needs only to say that the sentences (a) and (c) have the logical forms they appear to have. But anyone who denies either T1 or T3 has to give a different account.

A defender of the wide-scope theory has a ready reply. He can allow our intuitions of the mutual exclusiveness and joint exhaustiveness of the antecedent assumptions, but deny that there are only two assumptions involved in the contrast. If the "or" in (a) is a wide-scope conjunction, then to assert (a) is to assert the conjunction of the two conditionals

    (e) If *A* had been the case, then *C* would have been the case
    (f) If *B* had been the case, then *C* would have been the case

Hence, if we wish to make any assertion about what would have happened in any circumstances not covered (e) or (f) we have only one alternative to consider, namely, what would have happened if neither *A* nor *B* had been the case. The contrast is between two mutually exclusive and jointly exhaustive *sets* of assumptions. The wide-scope theorist can give a similar account of the contrast between (c) and (d). Anyone who asserts (c) is saying what would have happened under any of (possibly infinitely) many assumptions. And if he wished to say what would have happened under any circumstances other than those covered by (c), then he has only one alternative to consider, namely, what would have happened if nothing had been an *F*. The contrast is again between two mutually exclusive and jointly exhaustive sets of assumptions.

In moving from (a) to (b), or from (c) to (d) the scope and other changes occur because we are moving from considering what would have happened under any of a *set* of assumptions to considering what would have happened under one *particular* assumption, the singleton set on which complements the first set. And the negation operator is an appropriate device for effecting this change because of the mutual exclusiveness and joint exhaustiveness of the two sets in question.

Tentatively, then, my solution to the problem of simplification of disjunctive antecedents is to accept the wide-scope theory. In accepting this theory, one should be aware of some of its implications. All of the arguments which I have used here to defend the wide-scope theory can be applied, without doing anything except change the examples, to ordinary indicative conditionals. And one can look for no support from Japanese for treating the two kinds of conditionals differently in this respect. Hence, if an "or", occurring as the principal connective in the antecedent of a subjunctive conditional, is a wide-scope conjunction, then it is also a wide-scope conjunction in the antecedent of an indicative conditional.

Moreover, if the Japanese is any guide, then "or"s occurring in other contexts may be wide-scope conjunctions. The theory also implies that words like "anything" and "anyone" should not be considered to be existential quantifiers, but wide-scope universal quantifiers. Therefore, anyone who accepts the wide-scope theory will have to exercise some care in transcribing the sentences of natural languages into the symbolism of a formal language in which no wide-scope conjunctions or universal quantifiers occur. Alternatively, the formal languages might be enriched by including such conjunctions and quantifiers, and specifying the laws governing the structure of rational belief systems on such languages.

The wide-scope theory, which is proposed to solve the problem of simplification of disjunctive antecedents, is available to anyone who has a unified theory of conditionals. It does not depend on the adoption of any particular kind of semantics. But it would be *ad hoc* to apply it only to the analysis of subjunctive conditionals. If it applies at all, then there is no reason to suppose that it does not apply to indicative conditionals.

5. *The Probability of Conditionals*

The probability of conditionals presents problems for everyone. In this respect, it is like simplification of disjunctive antecedents. For the classical semanticist, the problem is that the probability of an indicative conditional behaves much more like a conditional probability than an absolute one for a material conditional, which, according to his theory, it should be.

For me, the problem is that it cannot actually *be* a conditional probability. If it were, then the classical probability calculus would provide at least the basis of an adequate logic of subjective probability for a language in which conditionals occurred, and the logical correspondence principle would be satisfied. However, Lewis has convincingly demonstrated that the probabilities of conditionals are not, in general, the corresponding conditional probabilities.[23]

In attempting to deal with *his* problem, Lewis has argued that a subjective probability evaluation on a conditional is not a measure of degree of belief, but of *degree of assertability*.[24] He claims that the degree of assertability of a conditional is the degree of belief in its truth minus a certain fraction of the degree to which its antecedent is believed to be false; this fraction being the ratio of the degree to which the conditional is believed to be false to that to which its antecedent is believed to be true. In justification of this claim, he says that a speaker ought not to assert a conditional, if he believes it to be true *predominantly because he believes its antecedent to be false*, because this would not only be pointless, but misleading. It would be pointless because he could simply deny the antecedent instead, and misleading because reasonable people might assume that he is not speaking pointlessly, and so must have some reason to believe the conditional to be true *over and above* his disbelief in its antecedent.

Given this argument, one would have expected Lewis to conclude that the degree of assertability $A(A \supset C)$ of a conditional $(A \supset C)$ is given by

(1) $A(A \supset C) = P(A \supset C) - P(\bar{A}) = P(AC)$

But instead, he subtracts from $P(A \supset C)$ only a fraction of $P(\bar{A})$, viz., $P(\bar{A}) \cdot P(\bar{C}A)/P(A)$, and so obtains

(2) $A(A \supset C) = P(A \supset C) - P(\bar{A}) \cdot P(\bar{C}A)/P(A) = P(C/A)$.

I cannot, as yet, see any justification for subtracting anything less than $P(\bar{A})$ from $P(A \supset C)$. However, assuming that there is a justification for diminishing $P(\bar{A})$ by the required fraction, as in (2), it follows that

(3) $A(\bar{A} \supset C) = P(C/\bar{A})$

But if the degrees of assertability of logically equivalent sentences are the same, then

(4) $A(A \lor C) = P(C/\bar{A}) = P(A/\bar{C})$

And this is so only if

(5) $P(A) = P(C)$

which is, surely, a very special case. Lewis is therefore committed to the view that logically equivalent sentences may have different degrees of assertability—even to those who are fully aware of their logical equivalence.

For this reason, I do not think that Lewis has yet solved his problem. Mine, on the other hand, is the problem of developing a satisfactory logic of subjective probability for a language which includes conditionals which will collapse into a satisfactory logic of truth and falsity claims on such a language when the range of possible probability values is restricted to 1 and 0. My starting point must be the requirements C13 and C14 on the structure of rational belief systems on languages with conditionals. For, what is required is a generalization of these requirements for degrees of belief other than, and including 1 and 0, from which these requirements may be derived as special cases.

Before proceeding with this, let us consider the three principal conditional logics, VW, VC and VCS. The differences between them are best brought out by some examples:

(1) If salt dissolves in water, then I had bacon and eggs for breakfast this morning.

Since both antecedent and consequent are true, anyone who accepts VC or VCS should consider (1) to be true. But one who thinks VW is the correct logic of conditionals may consider (1) to be false. Whether he did so would depend on what he thought should be included in his basis for reasoning from the supposition that salt dissolves in water. Is he to construct his basis for reasoning by feigning ignorance of the truth of the supposition and of other matters not in any way related to it? If so, then he will consider (1) to be false. Or, is he to retain, and include in his basis for reasoning from this supposition, the knowledge that he has of these other unrelated things? If so, then he will consider (1) to be true. Either way, it does not seem to matter very much what we say about (1). Normal intuition provides us with very little guidance concerning the acceptability or otherwise of conditionals with true antecedents and consequents which are epistemically and theoretically unrelated. The choice between VW and VC is, therefore, arbitrary.

The choice between VC and VCS, on the other hand, is more significant. Consider

> (2) If I had tossed this coin an hour ago, it would have landed heads, and
> (3) If I had tossed this coin an hour ago, it would not have landed heads.

According to Lewis, whose preferred system is VC, (2) and (3) are false. Both are false, because (presumably) there is no world in which both antecedent and consequent of (2) are true which is more like the actual world than any in which both antecedent and consequent of (3) are true, and conversely. But according to Stalnaker, who prefers VCS, one of (2) and (3) is true (but maybe we shall never know which), and the other is false. On this issue, I find both positions troublesome. I am troubled by Lewis' position, because I do not want to say that either (2) or (3) is false. It is not false that this coin would have landed heads if I'd tossed it, because, after all, it might have. It is a normal coin with heads on one side and tails on the other. And it is not false that it would not have landed heads, because it might well not have done so. Given what I know about this coin it seems that it would be just as wrong for me to assert of either (2) or (3) that it is false as it would be to assert of either that it is true. All I can reasonably claim is that each is probable to degree $\frac{1}{2}$.

Therefore, it seems that Stalnaker must be right. For, unlike Lewis, he is not committed to accepting or rejecting either of (2) or (3). He is committed to saying that one of (2) or (3) must *be* true and the other false. But this is compatible with his accepting that each is probable to degree $\frac{1}{2}$. Nevertheless, I am uneasy about Stalnaker's position too, because the concepts of truth and falsity do not rest easily with such conditionals. "Truth", here, cannot mean "corresponds to reality", unless there really is a unique possible world about which we are speaking in which the coin was tossed an hour ago. And it cannot mean "is ultimately rationally acceptable", or whatever it would have to mean on a coherence theory of truth, because there is no reason to suppose that either of (2) or (3) is ultimately rationally acceptable. Unless on examination it turns out that the coin is not, after all, a fair one, we probably know already almost as much as there is to know about the acceptability or otherwise of (2) or (3).

My uneasiness about regarding a probability claim concerning a conditional (whether it be an indicative or a subjunctive) as an expression of a degree of belief *in its truth* leads me to think that a far more radical approach to the theory of conditionals may eventually be required[25]—perhaps, one in which conditionals are regarded as a species of *indefinite propositions*, like "An arbitrarily selected A is a B", which, while it may be neither true nor false, may be probable to some degree.[26]

However, I do not wish to pursue this speculation here. I have mentioned it only to indicate the nature of my reservations concerning Stalnaker's position. Despite these reservations, I consider that Stalnaker's system, VCS, comes closest to a satisfactory logic of truth claims concerning conditionals. Accordingly, I shall take the requirements C13(a) and (b), C14(b) to (e), and the definition,

D4. $B_\alpha' = B_\alpha^+ + T\alpha$

where

(a) $T\beta \in B_\alpha^+$ if $T\Box\beta$ or $T(\alpha\Box\!\!\rightarrow\beta)$ occurs in B,
(b) $F\beta \in B_\alpha^+$ if $F(\alpha\Box\!\!\rightarrow\beta)$ occurs in B,
(c) B_α^+ is otherwise agnostic,

which serve to define the Stalnaker language, as my starting point for developing a logic of probability claims on conditionals.

Let LVCS be the Stalnaker language, so defined, and B any P-completable belief system on LVCS. Then the P-evaluations occurring in B must satisfy the axioms of the *absolute* probability calculus. In addition, by the logical correspondence principle, we must require that

CP13 (a) $P(\alpha\Box\!\!\rightarrow\beta) = 1$ in B only if $P\beta = 1$ in every member of $PE(B_\alpha')$
     (b) $P(\alpha\Box\!\!\rightarrow\beta) = 0$ in B only if $P\beta = 0$ in some member of $PE(B_\alpha')$

where $PE(B_\alpha')$ is the set of all P-completions of the base belief system B_α' which is derived from B by adjusting in some way the P-evaluations occurring in B so as to accommodate, if possible, $P\alpha = 1$. By the same principle we must also require that

CP14   (b) A member of $PE(B_\alpha')$ in which $P\beta = 1$ is a member of $PE(B_{\alpha\wedge\beta}')$

      (c) If some member of $PE(B_{\alpha\wedge\beta}')$ is a member of $PE(B_\alpha')$, then every member of $PE(B_{\alpha\wedge\beta}')$ is a member of $PE(B_\alpha')$

(d) If $B'_{\alpha \wedge \beta}$ is a rational belief system on LVCS, then so are B'_α and B'_β.

(e) $B'_\alpha = B$, if $P\alpha = 1$ in B.

And, in place of D4, we must have

DP4 $B'_\alpha =_{df} B^+_\alpha + T\alpha$

---

where

(a) $P\beta = 1$ in B^+_α if $P\square\beta$ or $P(\alpha\square\rightarrow\beta) = 1$ in B

(b) $P\beta = 0$ in B^+_α if $P(\alpha\square\rightarrow\beta) = 0$ in B

(c) $P\beta$ is unspecified in B^+_α if the P evaluation of β is not otherwise determined.

Given these requirements, we know that α is a valid *wff* of VCS iff $P\alpha = 1$ occurs in every P-completed belief system on LVCS.[27] The logical correspondence principle is therefore satisfied. What is needed now is a generalization of these requirements for i-th degree probability claims for $i < 1$. I suggest the following:

1. Replace CP13(b) by
   CP13 (c) $P(\alpha\square\rightarrow\beta) = in$ B only if $P\beta = i$ in some member of $PE(B'_\alpha)$, if $i < 1$.
2. Retain CP14(b) to (e) as they are.
3. Replace DP4(b) by
   DP4 (d) For $i < 1$, $P\beta = i$ in B^+_α if $P(\alpha\square\rightarrow\beta) = i$ in B.

From these new requirements, it follows that $P(\alpha\square\rightarrow\beta)$ behaves in most ways like the conditional probability $P(\beta/\alpha)$. In particular, if $P\alpha = 1$ in some rational belief system (i.e., if 'α' is not self-contradictory), then

PC1. $0 \leq P(\alpha\square\rightarrow\beta) \leq 1$

PC2. $P(\alpha\square\rightarrow(\beta\vee\sim\beta)) = 1$

PC3. $P(\alpha\square\rightarrow\beta) + P(\alpha\square\rightarrow\sim\beta) = 1$

PC4. $P(\alpha\square\rightarrow(\beta\vee\gamma)) = P(\alpha\square\rightarrow\beta) + P(\alpha\square\rightarrow\gamma) - P(\alpha\square\rightarrow(\beta\wedge\gamma))$.

The conjunction axiom is not provable, however, and in general $P(\alpha\square\rightarrow\beta)$ cannot be derived from $P\alpha$ and $P(\alpha\wedge\beta)$, even if $P\alpha \neq 0$. But in many cases, the probability of a conditional will be *contingently* the same as the corresponding conditional probability. In particular, if our P-evaluation of a conditional is independent of our *P*-evaluation of its antecedent, which is surely the normal case, then

$$P(\alpha \wedge \beta) = P(\alpha \wedge (\alpha \square \rightarrow \beta)) = P\alpha x P(\alpha \square \rightarrow \beta)$$

and in any such case

$$P(\alpha \square \rightarrow \beta) = P(\beta/\alpha) \text{ if } P\alpha \neq 0.$$

This is why the probability of a conditional normally behaves as though it were a conditional probability.

In general, the probability of a conditional cannot be independent of the probability of its antecedent; and this is really what Lewis has shown. That this is so can be illustrated by the following two sentences:

(1) He will be shot, if he will be shot if he confesses.
(2) He will be shot if he confesses.

Note that (2) is the antecedent of (1). Suppose we would assign a probability of 0.5 to his confessing and of 0.5 to his being shot. Then the probability we should assign to (1) is evidently a function of the probability which we should assign to (2). If we think (2) to be highly probable anyway, then the probability that he will be shot will not be much increased by the supposition that he will be shot if he confesses. If we think (2) to be highly improbable, then the probability that he will be shot will be greatly increased by the supposition that he will be shot if he confesses. Moreover, we may think that, in such a merciless regime, he will also be shot if he doesn't confess. Therefore, we may conclude that it is quite certain that he will be shot, if he will be shot if he confesses. The probability of (1) is, therefore, not independent of the probability of its antecedent. Therefore, the probability of the conjunction of (1) and (2) may not be equal to the product of the probabilities of (1) and (2). But the probability of the conjunction of (1) and (2) must be equal to the probability of

(3) He will be shot *and* he will be shot if he confesses.

Therefore, for the example, the conjunction theorem

$$P(\alpha \wedge \beta) = P\alpha x P(\alpha \square \rightarrow \beta)$$

fails.

NOTES

1. I have chosen to hang my objections on to realist "possible worlds" semantics for counterfactuals because I am convinced by Lewis' arguments that "every known way to explain away possible worlds turns out to appeal to analyticity" (Lewis (1973), p. 207). And this appeal immediately introduces the threat of circularity. For example, if possible worlds are defined to be maximally consistent sets of propositions (which is how Pollock (1976) defines them, (see p. 15)) then the threat emerges on two fronts. First, what is a proposition? If a proposition is a set of possible worlds (the set in which we should say that the proposition is true) then there has been no advance. If a proposition is an abstract third-world entity like a Fregean thought, there to be apprehended or not, then we might just as well buy realism about possible worlds. If it is a sentence of an idealized possible infinite language in which there are no ambiguities, no dependencies of meaning upon time or context of utterances, and no demonstratives or token reflexives, then we might just as well buy Fregean thoughts. Second, what is consistency? A consistent set of propositions is presumably a set of propositions all of which could be true. But how is the modality here to be defined if not in terms of possible worlds, and hence in terms of maximally consistent sets of propositions.

2. See Lewis (1973) for details.

3. The main reference is Stalnaker (1968).

4. See Chapter 4 of Lewis (1973).

5. I am not questioning that having true beliefs about counterfactual conditionals serves human interests. Obviously, to have knowledge of the generalized counterfactuals (laws) of science serves many such interests. My question is whether these instruments can be explained if a "possible worlds" account of counterfactuals is accepted.

6. See Davidson (1965).

7. In Goodman (1947).

8. I do not know how to make a clear distinction between truth and assertability conditions. There is an intuitive distinction between what I say (what belief I am purporting to express) and what I imply by how I say it (what beliefs it would be reasonable for others to assume I have, given that I have said what I have in the way that I have). For example, if I say "X happened on occasion O" then I am purporting to express a certain belief about the occasion O. And given that I have used the past tense, it would be reasonable for anyone to assume that I also believe O to be a past occasion. But this is not the belief that I purported to express, and the truth of the belief, which I purport to express by using this past-tense sentence, does not depend upon O being an occasion in the past. Had I said "X will occur on occasion O", while believing 'O' to be the name of a past occasion, I would have expressed the same belief concerning O, but I would have done so very misleadingly. To use the future tense in speaking about an occasion believed to be in the past is to violate an assertability condition. But the belief so expressed concerning this occasion may, nevertheless, be a true belief. (I am aware, of course, that this is not the usual way in which the distinction between truth and assertability conditions would be made. But it suits my purposes to make it this way, and I do not know of any objective basis for the distinction which would militate against my doing so.)

9. This objection was raised in Nute (1975), in Creary and Hill (1975) and in Fine (1975), and shown to be a serious objection in Ellis, Jackson and Pargetter (1977). A resolution of the difficulty was suggested in Loewer (1976). He claims that the problem arises as a result of confusing truth with assertability conditions. However, I think that this distinction is too unclear to bear the enormous weight which is now being put upon it. Every failure of standard logical theory to yield predictions which match our logical intuitions is being attributed to confusions about this distinction. For a discussion of the distinction see Brandom (1976).

10. See Chapter II, Section 7.

11. See Lewis (1973) §§1.7 and 6.1.

12. To prove this, it is sufficient to show that the axioms of VW are tautologies of LVW and that the rules of VW preserve tautologousness in LVW. To illustrate the method of proof, consider Lewis' long axiom:

A5. $((\alpha\square\rightarrow\sim\beta)\vee((\alpha\wedge\beta)\square\rightarrow\gamma)) \equiv (\alpha\square\rightarrow(\beta\supset\gamma))$

If A5 is not a tautology of LVW then there is a completed rational belief system B on LVW in which at least one of Case A, Case B or Case C occurs.

Case A
$T(\alpha\square\rightarrow\sim\beta)$
$F(\alpha\square\rightarrow(\beta\supset\gamma))$

For this B, there is no member of $E(B'_\alpha)$ in which $T\beta$ occurs. But there is some member of $E(B'_\alpha)$ in which both $T\beta$ and $F\gamma$ occur. *So not Case A.*

Case B
$T((\alpha\wedge\beta)\square\rightarrow\gamma)$
$F(\alpha\square\rightarrow(\beta\supset\gamma))$

For this B, there is no member of $E(B'_{\alpha\wedge\beta})$ in which $F\gamma$ occurs, and some member of $E(B'_\alpha)$ in which $T\beta$ and $F\gamma$ both occur. But any member of $E(B'_\alpha)$ in which $T\beta$ occurs is a member of $E(B'_{\alpha\wedge\beta})$. *So not Case B.*

Case C
$T(\alpha\square\rightarrow(\beta\supset\gamma))$
$F(\alpha\square\rightarrow\sim\beta)$
$F((\alpha\wedge\beta)\square\rightarrow\gamma)$

For this B, there is no member of $E(B'_\alpha)$ in which $T\beta$ and $F\gamma$ both occur; there is some member of $E(B'_\alpha)$ in which $T\beta$ occurs; and there is some member, say B^*, of $E(B'_{\alpha\wedge\beta})$ in which $F\gamma$ occurs. Therefore, some member of $E(B'_\alpha)$ is a member of $E(B'_{\alpha\wedge\beta})$, and hence $E(B'_{\alpha\wedge\beta})CE(B'_\alpha)$. Therefore, B^* is a member of $E(B'_\alpha)$ in which $T\beta$ and $F\gamma$ both occur. *So not Case C.*

13. See Chapter I, Section 5.

14. This has been argued in some detail in Ellis (1973).

15. See Section 5 below for a justification of this statement.

16. See Lewis (1976b) for details.

17. The logic of probability claims on conditionals is discussed more fully in Section 5 below.

18. If any violation of assertability conditions occurs in asserting (a) and denying (b) and (c), then I do not know where. One could assert (a) and deny (b) and (c) without having any idea where John lives.

19. The papers are Jackson (1977) and Lewis (1976a).

20. The counterexample is due to Adams (1970). The thesis I am defending was developed in Ayers (1965). Ayers claimed that "counterfactuality has no more to do with category than falsehood". (p. 365)

21. I owe this point to Frank Jackson.

22. I am grateful to Yoko Pinkerton for her efforts to explain the Japanese connectives to me.

23. In Lewis (1976b).

24. *Ibid.*, p. 298 and pp. 305-8.

25. For example, the kind of theory which is being developed in Adams (1975).

26. I made this suggestion in Ellis (1966) Chapter XI.

27. Since $P\alpha = 1$ occurs in any P-completed belief system on a language L iff $T\alpha$ occurs in every completed belief system on L.

Chapter IV

The Dynamics of Belief Systems

The laws of rationality which we have so far discussed are laws governing the structure of rational belief systems on languages containing various kinds of connectives and operators. They are, in a sense, *equilibrium laws*, because a rational belief system is conceived to be one which is in equilibrium under all pressures of internal criticism and discussion. But so far, we have said very little about the *dynamics* of belief systems, about how our belief systems evolve. The equilibrium laws do have dynamical implications. Newly acquired beliefs must be assimilated, modified or rejected if the system is to remain in (or be restored to) equilibrium. But presumably there are some specifically dynamical laws governing these processes.

From a knowledge of the law of conservation of energy, and of the mechanical equivalents of the various forms of energy, we may be able to say what changes in a given system are energetically possible. But until we know the laws of entropy, we are in no position to say how the system will change or respond to new energy inputs. Similarly, from a knowledge of the laws of logic, we may be able to say what kinds of rational belief systems on a language are logically possible. But until we know some laws more analogous to the laws of entropy we shall be in no position to say how a belief system will change, or be modified by new belief inputs.

For reasons which will become clearer, I do not believe that such laws are discoverable in the same kind of way as the laws of rational equilibrium. For these laws do not represent rational ideals, concerning the structure of belief systems on given languages, as the laws of logic do. The latter appeal to the normal intellect as ideals of rationality, are discoverable by introspection, and can be formulated as laws concerning rational belief systems on idealized formal languages. The former are principles which govern the growth and evolution of rational belief systems, are discoverable only after careful historical or psychological investigations (such as those of Kuhn or Piaget), and cannot be formulated as laws governing the growth and evolution of belief systems on idealized formal languages. The main reason why this is so is that questions about how our belief systems evolve cannot be separated from questions concerning the evolution of our language. The language we use to describe and to explain what is happening in the world reflects our theoretical understanding of it, and the language itself changes with changes in that theoretical understanding.

It is wrong to assume that our language exists preformed, as it were, and that the problem of how our belief systems evolve can be construed as one of how our belief systems on some given language become extended, or made more complete. For, our belief systems evolve, not merely by replacing some of the X evaluations on the sentences of a given language by T or F evaluations, but also by processes of conceptual revision.

Nevertheless, it is possible to say something about the dynamics of belief systems in advance of the detailed psychological and historical investigations which will eventually be required. It is possible to show that certain abstract principles of inductive reasoning, such as the straight rules of induction, are not the required principles. And it is possible to formulate some very general, although not very specific, laws of inductive projection which are concerned with the dynamics of rational belief systems.

1. *Inductive Scepticism*

In *A Treatise of Human Nature* and *Enquiry Concerning Human Understanding*, Hume divided the objects of all human knowledge into relations of ideas and matters of fact. He argued that our knowledge concerning relations of ideas is *a priori*, and that the required demonstrations concerning such relations could be carried out by *a priori* reasoning. It was not, for him, problematic how we could grasp, or recognize, the principles required for such demonstrations. His main concern was with our knowledge of matters of fact. What were the *a priori* principles which formed the bases of our reasoning concerning such matters? He argued persuasively, and some think conclusively, that there are no such principles, and that our knowledge of such matters is not based on reasoning, but on custom or habit.

We need not be too concerned with the amateur psychological theory which is involved in this claim. The processes by which we may come to believe statements concerning matters of fact may be much more complicated than those envisaged by Hume. His essential point, however, is that there is no *inductive logic*; there is only an *inductive psychology*. If Hume is right, then we shall search in vain for *a priori* inductive principles to serve as a foundation for reasoning concerning matters of fact. There are no such principles. We may hope to describe, more fully and accurately, the psychological processes involved in the acquisition of beliefs concerning matters of fact. But that is all.

I would agree with Hume, to the extent that I believe that there are no *a priori* principles of inductive reasoning. But then, since I do not believe that there are *any* such principles, inductive *or deductive*, I see no reason to dismiss inductive logic out of hand. For, presumably, the human brain is programmed to respond in certain sorts of ways to acquisitions of new beliefs, and there ought to be some principles governing such responses. The problem is to formulate laws governing *the dynamics* of human belief systems. Those we have so far formulated are not sufficiently determinative. Popper saw the point of Hume's essays very clearly, in making his distinction between the logic of knowledge and the psychology of knowledge, and in rejecting inductivism and justificationism.[1] But to my way of thinking, the logic of knowledge is just part of the psychology of knowledge, and hence I have no *theoretical* grounds for rejecting inductivism. It seems plausible that there should be principles of inductive projection concerned with the dynamics of rational belief systems, as well as principles governing the structure of rational belief systems in dynamic equilibrium.

I offer no solution to the problem of induction other than Hume's. But then, since I would offer an account of rationality very different from Hume's, I am not forced to the conclusion that our beliefs concerning matters of fact are not held rationally. For me, reasoning is not a matter of applying intuitively grasped *a priori* principles. It is a physical process which occurs in our heads, which, like other physical processes, is governed by physical laws. For me, the problem of induction is to specify these laws, and to demonstrate their capacity to explain certain dynamical properties of human belief systems. It is not to show how this or that change in any degree of belief can be justified by appeal to any *a priori*, or *a priori justifiable*, principles of inductive reasoning.

2. *On Vindicating Induction*[2]

Several notable attempts have been made in recent years to vindicate the straight rule of induction. I refer to Reichenbach's attempt to justify induction pragmatically,[3] and the later attempts of Salmon[4] to improve on Reichenbach's argument. These alleged pragmatic justifications of induction were attempts at *vindication* only—not *validation*. That is, the arguments did not claim to show that all, most, or even any, applications of the straight rule yield true predictions; they claimed only to show that use of the straight rule is the most rational policy. The arguments were intended to be deductive arguments from *a priori* premisses, which, if successful, would solve Hume's problem of induction, in a way which is consistent with the conception of man as a rational agent, applying (or perhaps misapplying) certain *a priori* (or *a priori justifiable*) principles of reasoning to immediately given data.

Very briefly, Reichenbach attempted to show:

(a) that there is a certain class of inductive rules (convergent rules) persistent use of which must eventually yield knowledge of probabilities, provided that such knowledge is attainable, and

(b) that there are no other rules which share this property.

He argued that since it is more rational to adopt a procedure which *must* eventually succeed in achieving our agreed aims (to attain knowledge of probabilities), if our aims are capable of achievement, than to adopt one which need not succeed in any circumstances, persistent use of convergent rules is vindicated.

As a vindication of induction, this argument has been seen to fall short on two counts. First, it does not succeed in selecting a *particular* inductive rule. Indeed, the class of inductive rules vindicated by Reichenbach's argument is so wide that every hypothesis concerning probabilities is consistent with some choice of convergent rule. Second, as probability is explicated by Reichenbach, the argument fails to show that knowledge of probabilities is worth having. For, if a probability is understood to be a limit of a potentially infinite sequence of relative frequency determinations (i.e., a long run relative frequency), it seems that knowledge of such limits can be of no real interest, unless we can be assured that these limits *are now being approached*. But then, it seems, in order to gain such assurance, we must already have solved the problem of *validating* induction. For, this assurance concerns our beliefs, not merely our methods.

We may put this second objection by saying that Reichenbach's vindication of induction fails to deal with the problem of *the short run*, which is, necessarily, our only real concern. The question of what may happen in the indefinite future may have a certain speculative and dreamy charm. But the only questions of real importance concern what is going to happen tomorrow, next year, or in the next couple of generations.

To meet these objections, Salmon has tried to show how the class of convergent rules could be narrowed down to the so-called *straight rule*: Estimate the long-run relative frequency to be equal to the observed relative frequency, and how one could construct an analogous argument to vindicate the *straight short-run rule*:[5] Estimate the relative frequency in any finite initial segment of a relative frequency sequence to be as near as possible to the (assumed known) long-run relative frequency. More recently, Lewis has argued that the straight rule is the only *immodest* inductive method, and that, when it comes to inductive methods, immodesty is a virtue.[6]

The details of these arguments need not concern us, since we may grant that they are sound. Nevertheless, we must be clear what they may legitimately be claimed to show. Reichenbach, Salmon and Lewis, in their different ways, have sought to narrow the class of permissible inductive rules by imposing certain *a priori* requirements on such rules; and each has concluded that the straight rules are the only ones which satisfy all of their requirements. Hence, *qua* rules of inductive projection, the straight rules have some desirable formal properties. However, this cannot be the whole story. For, where theories are involved, rational men do not justify their projections by appealing to the straight rules, and where theories are *not* involved, the straight rules can be used to justify any projection of any sequence.

1. On the first of these points, consider the simple case of tossing a coin, which we have examined carefully and found to be homogeneous in substance and symmetrical in figure. If 550 heads appeared in a sequence of 1000 throws, then the straight rule, ordinarily applied, would instruct us to predict that the long-run relative frequency of heads would be 55/100. But, even if no one had ever tossed a coin before, such a projection of the sequence would be considered absurd. For, in the first place, the occurrence of the observed sequence is in conformity with our present concepts of physical symmetry and mechanical causation (in the sense that it is the kind of result which is to be expected by anyone who shares our conceptual and theoretical framework). In the second place, the projected limit of 55/100 is inconsistent with this framework. For, if the limit, 55/100, were seriously entertained, some modification of currently accepted views of physical sym-

metry and/or mechanical causation must be envisaged. For example, we might have to suppose that facial markings affect mechanical behaviour. But this supposition would certainly have far-reaching theoretical repercussions. Therefore, we cannot accept the projected limit of 55/100, unless we are prepared to make radical revisions to our theoretical or conceptual framework.

It seems, therefore, that some restriction should be placed on the *range of applicability* of straight inductive rules. For, the above example suggests that the naive use of straight induction is not always the most rational policy.

It may be thought that, in this case, the use of straight induction is illegitimate, only because it fails to take into account the many other straight inductive arguments which might be brought to bear on the same issue. In other words, it might be suggested that, if due account were taken of these other (concatenated) arguments, a more acceptable conclusion would be reached. But this reply is demonstrably unsatisfactory. For,

(1) Scientific theories have a legitimate role in determining what probability estimates we should make (i.e., it is at least sometimes rational to be guided by scientific theories in making predictions),

(2) There are no determinative rules for scientific theory construction (i.e., there are no rules which determine *uniquely* what theory should be constructed on the basis of what supposedly known facts about particulars), and

(3) An inductive rule is a determinative rule for making probability estimates *solely* on the basis of supposedly known facts about particulars.

Therefore,

(4) Not all rationally made probability judgements can be adequately justified by reference to inductive rules and supposedly known facts about particulars.

Hence, no vindication of induction which succeeds only in showing the rational preferability of using certain inductive rules can possibly solve the general problem of vindicating scientific inductive practices. At best, it can only demonstrate the rational preferability of using these rules *where there are no relevant theoretical considerations*. In other words, the most that a pragmatic justification of induction can possibly do is show the rational preferability of using certain inductive rules to make probability estimates concerning things which are *theoretically isolated.*

2. The second point was that where the objects of our probability judgements are theoretically isolated, straight inductive rules can be used to justify any projection of any sequence. Consequently, where there is *no* relevant background of theory, every projection is as good or as bad as every other, and no *satisfactory* justification can be provided for any inductive projection. Moreover, it is possible to show this *without* introducing such odd predicates as 'grue' and 'bleen', as Goodman did in making a similar point.[7] Hence our practices of inductive projection cannot possibly be justified by any theory of *predicate-entrenchment*, as Goodman hoped.[8]

Suppose that a computer is turning up numbers on a screen, and that the first five numbers to appear are 1, 2, 3, 4, 5, in that order. An observer will naturally expect that if the computer continues to operate, the numbers 6, 7, 8, ... will subsequently appear on the screen in serial order. But what is the rational basis for this expectation? Let us suppose that our observer has read Reichenbach's and Salmon's arguments and has become convinced that using straight inductive rules is the only rationally justifiable inductive policy. Is he, even so, in any position to justify the actual use that he makes of these rules? Of course, he may argue that since in each case $\alpha_n = n$, where α_n is the nth number to appear on the screen, then in future too, $\alpha_n = n$. And, since this accords with the inductive policy which is rationally preferable to all others, this is the most rational prediction that can be made in the circumstances. However, he could equally well argue that since in each case

$$\alpha_n = (n-1)\,(n-2)\,(n-3)\,(n-4)\,(n-5)+n$$

where α_n is the nth number to appear on the screen, then, in future too,

$$\alpha_n = (n-1)\,(n-2)\,(n-3)\,(n-4)\,(n-5)+n$$

And, this prediction also accords with straight inductive policy.

Hence, if the prediction $\alpha_6 = 6$ is rationally preferable, on straight inductive grounds, so also is the prediction $\alpha_6 = (5!+6) = 126$. Indeed, it is not difficult to show that there are infinitely many predictions that can be made, strictly in accordance with straight inductive policies, all mutually incompatible. That being the case, the mere assurance that straight inductive rules are rationally preferable to others, does nothing to vindicate the use that we make of these rules, at least, in the kind of case envisaged.

Now, the logical situation is not changed, if in place of 1, 2, 3, 4, 5, the computer throws up the numbers 1, 1, 1, 1, 1. We can argue that since in each case $\alpha_n = 1$, so in general $\alpha_n = 1$. But we can also argue that since in each case

$$\alpha_n = (n-1)\,(n-2)\,(n-3)\,(n-4)\,(n-5) + 1$$

so, in general,

$$\alpha_n = (n-1)\,(n-2)\,(n-3)\,(n-4)\,(n-5) + 1.$$

Hence, the prediction $\alpha_6 = 1$ is no better placed than the prediction $\alpha_6 = 121$.

Again, the logical situation is apparently not changed essentially, if in place of the computer sequence, we consider any natural sequence of events. Suppose, for example, that instead of watching numbers thrown onto a screen, we are observing the variations in brightness of a Cepheid Variable star (the first ever observed) and measuring the time-intervals t_n from maximum to maximum. Tabulating our results, we might obtain the sequence:

$$t_1 = 4 \text{ days}$$
$$t_2 = 4 \text{ days}$$
$$t_3 = 4 \text{ days}$$
$$t_4 = 4 \text{ days}$$
$$t_5 = 4 \text{ days}$$

If we can argue that $t_6 = 4$ days on the basis of straight induction, we can also argue that $t_6 = 124$ days on precisely the same grounds. For while it is true that for each n ($n=1$ to $n=5$), $t_n = 4$ days, it is also true that for each n ($n=1$ to $n=5$),

$$t_n = ((n-1)\,(n-2)\,(n-3)\,(n-4)\,(n-5) + 4) \text{ days.}$$

It is obvious that similar considerations would apply to any set of quantitative results. The actual length of the sequences considered is quite irrelevant to the structure of the argument. For the plain mathematically demonstrable fact is that any finite initial segment of a sequence can be continued in infinitely many ways, provided only that there is no prior constraint on the complexity of the generating functions that may be employed. Consequently, unless we are prepared to supplement the straight rules of induction by some other principles or rules (such as a principle of simplicity), the knowledge that we are to use only straight rules of induction can give us no guidance at all in making quantitative predictions.

Now what applies to quantitative results also applies to non-quantitative ones. The fact that the first n members of a given sequence of objects all possess the property P need not imply (even according to straight inductive canons) that the next member of the sequence α_{n+1} will also possess the property P. For the sequence of results α_1 is P, α_2 is P, α_3 is P, ..., α_n is P can be continued in any way we please, and whatever way we choose, there will be an appropriate rule to generate the extended sequence.

Thus, the prediction α_{n+1} is Q might be justified in the following way. Suppose that when the first result α_1 is P is obtained, the sequence of results α_2 is P, α_3 is P, ..., α_n is P, α_{n+1} is Q, α_{n+2} is Q, ... is *envisaged*. Then in each case, up to α_n is P, the results obtained would be seen *to conform to the envisaged sequence*. They would be seen to be alike in this respect. Consequently, we should, entirely in accordance with straight inductive rules, predict that in future too the results obtained will conform to this sequence. Consequently, we should predict that α_{n+1} *is Q*.

It follows, quite generally, that the Reichenbach-Salmon vindications of straight-induction would not, even if they were completely successful in achieving their aims, justify any *actual* inductive practices. It is one thing to offer an *a priori* justification for an abstractly formulated inductive rule, and another to justify any actual piece of reasoning which might be seen as being an application of that rule. The pragmatic justifications of induction fail in this way.

3. *The Importance of Theories*

Consider the sequence of cases discussed in the last section. It will be noticed that the "odd" applications of straight inductive rules seem to become progressively more irrational. Intuitively, at least, that is what we would say. In the first computer case, for example, we should not be greatly astonished to find the number 126 appear on the screen immediately after the number 5. After all, we know that computers can be programmed to generate extremely complex sequences, and it would not conflict with anything else we think we know about the world to suppose that the computer has indeed been programmed to generate a complex sequence which happens to begin: 1, 2, 3, 4, 5, ...

Of course, we might argue that there are limits to the

complexity of the sequences which even computers are able to generate. Moreover, even if there were no such limits, extremely complex sequences like those described are neither mathematically nor physically interesting and, hence, are unlikely to be programmed for any purpose other than trickery. In other words, we might attempt to justify our expectation that the sequence, 1, 2, 3, 4, 5, will be continued 6, 7, 8, ... in terms of the psychology and interests of computer programmers. Even so, it would lead to no basic conflict with our understanding of the world to suppose that the sequence, 1, 2, 3, 4, 5, would indeed continue, 126, 727, ... and so on.

In this sense, then, the computer sequences are *theoretically isolated*. If it were not for such incidental information as we may possess concerning the structure of computers, and the interests of computer programmers, we should, indeed, have no grounds whatever for preferring one continuation of the sequence to any other.

The theoretical isolation of the computer sequence (which admittedly is imperfect) stands in striking contrast to the theoretical involvement of what I have called natural sequences. For all that the use of straight inductive rules can tell us, the sequence of time-interval measurements (between maxima in star brightness variations) might be expected to continue in any way at all. But if the sequence were in fact to continue in some "irregular" fashion (that is, in a way that is radically different from what we should ordinarily expect), this would at once pose an immense theoretical problem.

So long as the sequence is "regular", we can see that a detailed quantitative explanation might be forthcoming in terms of accepted laws and theories. Perhaps, we do not yet have a completely satisfactory explanation of the variations in brightness of Cepheid Variables. Nevertheless, the law of brightness variation that we suppose applies to these stars is such that we are able to imagine several possible explanations conforming to accepted laws and theories. But if the law of brightness variation were highly complex, it would be difficult to suggest *any* hypotheses compatible with accepted laws and theories which could possibly lead to the generation of such a sequence. Hence, we must contemplate the possibility that extraordinary laws, quite unlike any others known to us, are involved in the detailed explanation. Either that, or else that our theoretical picture of stellar constitution is grossly inaccurate. We might, for example, contemplate the possibility that stars have a structure comparable in complexity and organization to a computer. But in any case we must consider making radical revisions or additions to the structure of our physics.

Now, if a sequence of events, physically so isolated as the brightness variations of a distant star, is so heavily involved theoretically, the contrast between theoretical isolation and theoretical involvement is even more striking when we turn to consider more everyday sequences. The discovery of a substance which, chemically and physically, possessed all of the known characteristics of lead but which, spectrographically, was utterly different from lead would have far-reaching though unforeseeable theoretical repercussions. If green things everywhere turned blue, and blue things green, we should be completely at a loss to account for such happenings. (That is, if things really were discovered to be grue and bleen, the ramifications of this discovery would extend throughout physics, chemistry, and physiology.) If the length of the day, as measured on ordinary clocks, suddenly began to show enormous variations, this too would have shattering theoretical consequences.

Clearly, if sufficiently many such devastating things were actually to occur, our theoretical understanding of the world would be destroyed, and, for a time at least, anyone's guess as to what would then happen would be as good as anyone else's. Science can take a few shocks; but after sufficiently many, they would cease even to be shocks. For the scientific structure, against which they appeared as shocks, would cease to exist.

In any world where such things have actually occurred in sufficient number, rational argument concerning future contingencies would become impossible. Sequences would occur, but they would have lost their theoretical involvement. Consequently, we should all be in the position of the man watching the computer. Indeed, our position would be somewhat worse than his, since we should have no knowledge of the structure of the computer, or of the interests of computer operators. In a world where every sequence is theoretically isolated from every other, every projection into the future is as sound as every other.

We may, therefore, conclude that *theoretical involvement is a necessary condition for rational non-demonstrative argument.* This is really the lesson to be learned from the Goodman paradoxes. The paradoxes arise only because we vaccillate in our way of regarding such terms as "emeralds" and "green." Thus, on the one hand, we are invited (by Goodman in presenting his example) to agree that all evidence that emeralds are green is, at the same time, evidence that all emeralds are grue. (To comply, we must take "evidence" to mean "straight inductive evidence", and we must disregard the theoretical commitments made by the use of the terms "emeralds" and "grue.") On the other hand, it is suggested that the conclusion that the next emerald to be observed will be found to be blue is absurd. (But it is so only if "emeralds" and "blue" are *not* taken to be meaningless, theoretically uncommitted terms, but to refer to a certain kind of *stone* and a certain *colour* respectively.)

4. *Laws of Inductive Projection*

I conclude from the arguments of the previous two sections that the laws of inductive projection cannot be inductive rules of the kind they are traditionally supposed to be. That is, they cannot be rules for estimating probabilities solely on the basis of supposedly known facts about particulars. The probability estimates a rational man would make would have to depend on what theories he held, and if, *as is impossible*, he held no theories at all, then he could make no specific estimates. I say that this is impossible because the process of learning a language is a theory-learning process. One cannot become a competent speaker of a natural language without coming to share at least some of the common precepts of the language community. One must, for example, have some concept of causal influence to distinguish between "John is lifting a boulder in his hands" and "John has his hands underneath an elevated boulder." And one must have a concept of an enduring object to understand the sentence "This is the man I met yesterday."

Inductive projection from supposedly known facts about particulars often appears *not* to depend on any background theory, because the theory, upon which our understanding of the statements reporting the supposedly known facts is based, is often not articulated. It is absorbed in learning the language, and presupposed by the statements we should make in reporting these supposed facts. But, if the claims of the previous two sections are sound, then a rational man can make no inductive projections at all from theoretically isolated material. He must have some theoretical views about the nature of the things he is talking about and of the properties he is attributing to them. Consequently, there can be no abstract inductive principles of the kind envisaged by Carnap. $P(Fa_{n+1}/(Fa_1 \wedge Fa_2 \wedge \ldots \wedge Fa_n))$ can have any value at all for a rational man, depending on the nature of the subject matter and the theories he holds.

A rational man starts from where he is in making predictions about the future. That is, he projects from the basis of his total corpus of beliefs. He does not, and cannot, put his total theoretical understanding of the world aside to project from a supposedly neutral basis of observation statements. There is no such basis. And even if there were, he could not do it. For, given such a basis, any projection would be as good as any other.

The question, then, is how he proceeds from where he is. It follows, from what has been said in Section 3, that his methodology, in making predictions and projections, must be *theoretically conservative*. That is, he will not make projections which, if believed, would undermine his theoretical understanding of the world. It cannot be rational to reject any theory that one holds *solely* on the basis of projections. For if it were, then all theories could be rejected out of hand, and we should have no basis for making any projections at all. To illustrate, consider once again the coin-tossing case. In the imagined experiment, the result obtained of 550 heads in 1000 throws is of the kind one would expect, given our theories about physical symmetry, mechanical causation and random variations. There is no conflict here with our theoretical expectations. However, to project a long-run relative frequency of 55/100 would be incompatible with these expectations. Therefore, if we seriously believed this projection, we should have to consider revising our theories, and hence our theoretical understanding of the world, *not* as a result of what has happened, but because of what we are projecting *will* happen. Now this, I contend, is irrational, because if our thought processes actually operated in this way, we should rapidly reach a standpoint from which we should be powerless to form *any* rational expectations.

My first law of inductive projection, then, is *the principle of theoretical conservatism: A rational man anticipates that what will happen (or what will be found to have happened) will be as much in accord with his theoretical understanding of the world as what he already believes to have happened.* This is not, of course, to say that he is a dogmatist about his theories. It is only to say that *if* he has no reason to doubt his theoretical understanding of the world, then he will not make projections which, if substantiated, would bring them into doubt. Consider the "grue" paradoxes again. All observed emeralds have been green. Therefore, all observed emeralds are either green and have been observed or blue and have not been observed. Let "grue" abbreviate this complex predicate. Then it is true that all observed emeralds are grue. But the projection that all emeralds are grue, and hence that all unobserved emeralds are blue is not a rational projection for anyone whose theoretical understanding of the world is anything like ours. For to accept this projection would be to reject our physical theories and/or our theories of colour and observation, not on the basis of what has been observed, but entirely on the basis of our projections about what will be observed, contrary to the principle of theoretical conservatism.

I cannot rule out, *a priori,* the possibility of a rational man having a bizarre theoretical understanding of the world with which this particular projection is compatible. For him, such a projection would be a rational one. I cannot imagine the framework he would have to have for such a projection to be rational, but if anyone has such a framework, then let him come forward and try to convince us that his way of viewing the world is preferable to ours. If he can do so, then he will have changed our standards of rationality. For, he will have changed our views about the inferences it is rational to make from the evidence that all observed emeralds are green (or grue).

The question of what inferences can rationally be drawn from what evidence is thus not a question which can be settled by appeal to any *a priori* principles of inference. It depends on the theoretical standpoint from which the evidence is viewed. But presumably, not all theoretical standpoints are equally good. Presumably, some are better than others. And presumably, it is rational to try to *improve* one's theoretical understanding of the world. The principle of theoretical conservatism cannot, therefore, be more than part of the story. It may be rational to start from where one is, and to be guided by one's theories in making projections, but surely a rational man will, at the same time, seek to make his theories better.

What, then, makes one theory better than another, and what principles of rationality govern the improvement of theoretical understanding? We may gain some guidance concerning these two questions by reconsidering the argument for theoretical conservatism. Theoretical involvement, we argued, is a necessary condition for the possibility of rational projection, and theoretical conservatism is a necessary condition for the maintenance of theoretical involvement. But, as we have seen, there are grades of theoretical involvement. The computer sequences, discussed in Section 2, are less theoretically involved than the natural sequences we discussed. And, as the theoretical involvement becomes less, the range of compatible projections increases, and hence the degree of uncertainty in our projections increases. Therefore, for anticipating nature, *we require theories which will narrow as much as possible (without eliminating) the range of compatible projections of accepted data.*

Consider again the computer sequence which begins 1, 2, 3, 4, 5, ... To project this sequence, we need a theory about what is going on. Perhaps the computer operator is generating the numeral sequence. Perhaps he is doing a programme for *Sesame Street*, and generating the sequence, 1, 2, 3, 4, 5, 6, 7, 8, 9, 10, 10, 9, 8, 7, 6, 5, 4, 3, 2, 1. There are dozens of such more or less plausible hypotheses. To arrive at a theory, a rational man will seek to eliminate some of these alternatives by waiting a bit longer to see what will happen, or by seeking information about the occasion of the computer's programming, or the interests and aims of the computer's programmer. At this stage, his enquiry will involve neither conjectures nor refutations. His aim is to *arrive at* a conjecture, not to test one. He requires a theory which accords with the background theories and information he has about people and computers, which accounts for the data he has, which is compatible with any additional information he has been able to gather about the case, and which narrows as much as possible the range of projections of the sequences which might compatibly be made. A rational man, who has an interest in knowing what will happen, will seek such a theory.

It also follows from the necessity for theoretical involvement that rational men will seek to extend their theories to cover as wide a range of phenomena as possible. For, where any given subject matter remains theoretically isolated (or relatively so) we are powerless to make (or less capable of making) projections or predictions concerning it. A rational man will therefore seek to increase theoretical involvement by making his theories as comprehensive in their application as possible.

These two observations lead me to what I shall call *the principle of theory development: A rational man strives to develop a theoretical understanding of the world which is as precise in the predictions it yields, and as comprehensive in its application is possible.*

It is evident that this principle is closely related to Popper's claim that rational men should aim to increase the *degree of falsifiability* of their theories as much as possible[9] (without actually rendering them inconsistent). In spirit, I agree with Popper. But, I would not call it a "degree of falsifiability" which he is seeking to maximize because that would wrongly suggest that a rational man will reject a theory whose predictions are not substantiated. And this is not my position. On the contrary, given the need to maintain theoretical involvement, *a rational man will stick to theories, which he considers to have proven worth, as best he can, until he can come up with something better.*[10] For, it is better to have some, even if not entirely satisfactory means of anticipating nature, than none at all. A rational man, who is lost in the scrub, will prefer to follow a path which is ill-defined and strewn with obstacles, than to strike out into the bush. But, he will be on the lookout for, and willing to explore, any more promising paths he may happen to come across.

These principles of inductive projection are, of course, vague and ill-defined, and presumably very incomplete. If I had to be more specific, I would go for a methodology of scientific research programmes very like that of Imre Lakatos.[11] But I would not think of it as a *methodology*, because that suggests that we are free to accept or reject it as we will. If I am right then we have no such choice to make. Rational men think as they do, because they have no choice in the matter; and the problem is to formulate an ideal of rational thought which can be used to account for the facts of our scientific, cultural and personal histories, and which at the same time functions, for the normal intellect, as a regulative ideal.

NOTES

1. See Popper (1934), p. 30.
2. This section and the following one are revised versions of sections 1 and 2 of Ellis (1965b).
3. Reichenbach (1938), Sec. 42, and (1935), Sec. 87.
4. Salmon (1961), pp. 245–64.
5. See Salmon (1955).
6. Lewis (1971). But see also Spielman (1972) and Lewis (1974).
7. Goodman (1955), Ch.3.
8. Ibid., Ch. 4.
9. Popper (1934), Ch. 6.
10. Kuhn (1962) and Kuhn in Lakatos and Musgrave (1970), pp. 1–24 and 231–78.
11. Lakatos (1970).

CONCLUSION

In this essay, I have tried to show that the laws of logic are laws governing the structure of rational belief systems on idealized languages. I have argued that these laws are not *a priori* principles which we, as rational agents, are somehow able to grasp, and apply in reasoning about things. Rather, they have a status similar to the laws of mechanics. The latter apply directly only to idealized entities, such as mass-points in inertial systems; but they provide a framework for explaining the behaviour of ordinary physical objects in ordinary physical systems. The laws of logic, likewise, apply directly only to the idealized constituents of ideally rational belief systems; but they provide a framework for explaining some of the structural and dynamical features of ordinary human belief systems.

The laws of logic, I have argued, are equilibrium laws. They describe the structural properties of ideal belief systems in rational equilibrium, i.e., in equilibrium under all pressures of internal criticism and discussion. Ordinary belief systems will rarely, if ever, achieve such an equilibrium state, partly because of the entry, through experience, of new beliefs into these systems, and partly because the required pressures are not applied. But if human beings aspire to have belief systems which would be in equilibrium under such pressures, the rational ideal will appear not only as a *physical* ideal, which can be used to explain some of the structural and dynamical properties of our belief systems, but also as a *regulative* ideal.

The theory here developed may justly be called *psychologistic*. But it is not the crude psychologism of which everyone is so rightly disparaging. It flows from a more sophisticated view about the nature of many scientific laws than any which was defended, or even conceived of, by writers, such as Mill, who espoused the cruder form of psychologism which was current in the last century. For me, scientific laws are generally framework principles, providing idealizations of behaviour, against which actual behaviour may be measured or compared. As framework principles, they determine what we shall regard as an effect. For, an effect is just a difference between actual and idealized behaviour. Consequently, the framework principles determine a research programme—to explain why things do not behave in the way that they would if they were ideal. My contention is that the laws of logic are like this. Insofar as a human belief system is, or is apparently not logically structured, this presents a problem for explanation. Perhaps we have misunderstood, perhaps the subject has changed his mind between utterances, perhaps he has his own ideolect, perhaps he is drawing attention to some ambiguity of the language by speaking paradoxically, perhaps he has not seen the connection, and so on—all testable hypotheses. If we fail to find such an explanation, and if this happens sufficiently often, and apparently systematically, then perhaps we should look again at our logical principles. In this way, our logical principles, like any other of the framework principles of science, could come to be revised.

By the laws of logic, I mean such statements as "There is no rational belief system on the language L_0 in which any sentence of the form "$\alpha \lor \sim \alpha$" occurs with an F evaluation", or "If B is a rational belief system on a language L, then B is completable through every extension of L." These statements are about belief systems in the sense in which, say, Newton's First-Law of Motion is a statement about how bodies move. Fully articulated, Newton's First Law is that every mass-point, which is not subject to the action of any forces, continues in its state of rest or uniform motion in a straight line relative to absolute space. This law is quite obviously not just a generalization about how actual bodies move. Nor does it become so, if we refer the motion, not to absolute space, but to any arbitrary inertial system. It remains a framework law, useful *in the process of explaining* how actual bodies move, but not descriptive of their motion. Similarly, the laws of logic do not describe the structure of any actual belief systems. But they are useful, all the same, for explaining their structure. The mistake, both of earlier psychologistic theorists, and of their critics, was to suppose that the laws of thought had to be true generalizations about how people think. For them, the paradigm of a scientific law was a statement like "All crows are black." I do not think that I need to dwell on the absurdity of this. But it is perhaps worth remarking that this naive theory about the nature of scientific laws is not yet dead. There are still those who believe that an extensional language will ultimately prove to be adequate for all of the purposes of science. And this could only be the case if the ultimate laws of science are true universal generalizations.

It should be clear that by "the laws of logic" I do not mean such sentences of an idealized formal language as "$p \lor \sim p$." Such a sentence is no more an expression of a law than the equation "$\frac{dy}{dt} = 0$", or "$f = \frac{d(mv)}{dt}$." We may indeed be able to refer to a law by citing such an expression or equation. But the law referred to is a statement, expressible in a natural language, about what holds in some kind of idealized system.

To establish the view I hold concerning the nature of the laws of logic, it is not enough to show that the critiques of naïve psychologism are themselves based on a naïve conception of scientific laws. It has to be shown that a theory of rational belief systems can be developed which will do the job which in the past has been done by theories of truth, *viz* provide semantic foundations for logical systems. I have, accordingly, sought to formulate some laws of logic, governing the structure of rational belief systems on various kinds of formal languages, which will do precisely this. And, I think I have succeeded in showing how such foundations can be provided for most of the standard logical systems, including the sentential and lower predicate calculi, the standard modal sentential and predicate logics, the most commonly accepted logics of conditionals, and various combinations of these. In each case, I have tried to formulate the most primitive logical laws which will yield the required system.

A set of logical laws describing the structure of a rational belief system on a syntactically, but otherwise only implicitly defined formal language, yields a logical system in the sense that it determines what sentences of the language may or may not occur with T or F evaluations in a rational belief system on the language. Those which cannot occur with an F evaluation in any rational belief system on the language may be said to be tautologies of the language. The logical system yielded by a given set of rationality requirements (i.e., logical laws) concerning belief systems on a language is the set of all tautologies of that language.

The foundations for logical systems, which are thus provided, by-pass theories of truth. They do so in the sense that they leave open the question of whether any sentence of a given language can be said to be true or false in an objective sense. And this is surely as it should be. The fact that we can have a rational system of beliefs about what ought or ought not morally to be done, does not imply that moral judgements are objectively true or false. In defining a rational belief system on a language, no assumption need be made that any sentence of the language is objectively true or false. This may, or may not be so, depending on the language in question. But surely we do not need to assume that it is so, when judging whether a given belief system on the language is rational. Our theory of rationality ought not to depend on any theory of truth. My main criticism of classical semantics is that it ties the concept of rationality to a particular theory of truth, which is fine for first order predicate calculus, but not much good for anything else. For, in order to describe adequate classical semantics for modal and conditional logics, it turns out to be necessary to postulate the existence of an infinity of possible worlds related to each other in various ways, and populated (some of them) by counterparts of people and objects in this world.

Heuristically, this hypothesis has been extremely fruitful, and many beautiful results and elegant proofs have been obtained by means of it. But philosophically, it has not produced much enlightenment. We know much more about the complex networks of modal and conditional logical systems, how to axiomatise them, provide completeness proofs for proposed axiom systems, and so on. But none of this has helped us to understand the rôles of modalities and conditionals in human thought and discourse. Nor has it helped us to see how human beings can acquire the language skills necessary for such thought or discourse. The claim that something is necessarily true is supposed to be the claim that it is true at all worlds accessible to the actual world. What kind of claim it is, is supposed to depend on the nature of this accessibility relationship. But we are given no way of discovering or investigating accessibility relationships, and it remains a mystery how anyone could come to accept or understand any kind of necessity claim.

On the semantics for modal logics here presented, the analogue of a possible world turns out to be a completed belief system. The analogue of the set of possible worlds accessible to a given world turns out to be the set of completed extensions of a belief system B' which is defined in relationship to the belief system B which corresponds to the given world. The formal properties of the accessibility relationship bepend on how B' is defined in relation to B for the language in question. Intuitively, B' can be thought of as a kind of hard core within a system of beliefs which is being retained as a basis for hypothetical reasoning in some context of discussion or enquiry. What we should include in B' depends on the kind of enquiry we are making. Given this account, it is not hard to see how the use of modalities can come to be learned and understood. The accessibility relationships can be discovered by considering what principles are operative in determining the contents of the base belief system B' in the particular context in which the modalities are being used.

The semantics I propose for conditionals are formally similar to the semantics for modal logics. But, instead of a base belief system B', which is fixed for the whole context of discussion or enquiry, we consider a different basis for each distinct antecedent of the conditionals we are concerned with. Thus, for a conditional whose antecedent is 'α', we consider a base belief system B'_α which, besides $T\alpha$, includes every belief which we should retain, or additionally suppose, when reasoning from the supposition that α. The kind of conditional logic we obtain then depends on how B'_α is defined in relation to B. If $B'_\alpha = B + T\alpha$, the conditional is a material conditional. If $B'_\alpha = B' + T\alpha$, it is a strict conditional of some kind. If $B'_\alpha = B^+_\alpha + T\alpha$, it is a Stalnaker conditional. If $B'_\alpha = B^*_\alpha + T\alpha$, it is a variably strict-conditional of some kind, depending on what other requirements are made on bases for hypothetical reasoning from a given supposition.

There are, of course, analogues of possible worlds here too, and analogues of nearness relationships between them. A completed belief system B is the analogue of a possible world W. The set of completed extensions, $E(B'_\alpha)$, of B'_α is the analogue of the set, W_α, of α-worlds nearest to W. The formal properties of the relationships between B and the members of $E(B'_\alpha)$ are determined by the requirements on B'_α. Hence, these same requirements also determine the relationships between W and the members of W_α. Therefore, we can know about these relationships once we know how to form B'_α from B, which is what we learn when we learn to suppose.

The theory of rational belief systems thus provides foundations for all of the standard logical systems, and does so without reliance upon any theory of truth. Moreover, foundations for modal and conditional logics can be provided without postulating, or even pretending, that there are possible worlds other than the actual world. What the theory does is to show that if rational belief systems on certain formal languages (which are constructed to model certain features of natural languages), are postulated to satisfy certain primitive requirements (suggested by the intended interpretation of the model), then there are certain sentences of these formal languages (the tautologies) which cannot occur with F evaluations in any rational belief systems upon them.

The theory of rational belief systems is therefore something more than just a promise. It provides an alternative to classical semantics, which is evidently no less powerful than the theory it is intended to replace. The two theories may therefore be compared on other grounds. Concerning the sentential and first order predicate languages there is little to choose between the two theories. Classical semantics provides as good an explanation as any of the structure of rational belief systems on such languages. Classical semantics is at home in this area. But when it comes to modal and conditional languages, the case is otherwise. Classical semantics for these languages present a pervasive air of artificiality, which one cannot help being struck by. I am reminded of Duhem's reaction to Oliver Lodge's theory of electricity.[1]

> "Here is a book (O. Lodge, op. cit.) intended to expound the modern theories of electricity and to expound a new theory. In it there are nothing but strings which move around pulleys, which roll around drums, which go through pearl beads, which carry weights; and tubes which carry water while others swell and contract; toothed wheels which are geared to one another and engage hooks. We thought we were entering the tranquil and neatly ordered abode of reason, but we find ourselves in a factory."

And my reaction to classical semantics for modal and conditional languages is somewhat similar. Of course, I cannot prove that possible worlds, other than this one, do not exist, or are not related in the kinds of ways they are supposed to be to the actual world. But I see no reason whatever to suppose that they do, or that it is worthwhile *pretending* they do. On the contrary, they give every appearance of being, like Lodge's pulleys and strings, fictions invented to satisfy the requirements of an untenable theoretical viewpoint. In Lodge's case it was the mechanistic world view. In the present case, it is the identification of semantics with truth theory.

The one great advantage which I would claim for the theory of rational belief systems over classical semantics, is that it can be used to provide foundations for modal and conditional logics without any of this air of artificiality. Of course, my formal languages, and rational belief systems, are artificial in a sense. For, they are idealizations of natural languages and belief systems. There are difficulties here, no doubt. But every science contains such idealizations, and it is no criticism of science of human thought that it should do likewise. But possible worlds are not idealizations of anything. They are much more like Lodge's strings and pulleys. Even if they are taken only half seriously, they are still an essential part of the theory.

A good theory should have some spin-offs. One spin-off from the theory of rational belief systems is that it can easily be extended to provide foundations for logics of probability claims. One only has to consider T and F evaluations to be limiting probability evaluations (of 1 and 0), introduce a notion of P-completability analogous to that of completability, and generalize the rationality requirements to cover intermediate P-evaluations on the sentences of a given language, to obtain a logic of probability claims on that language which satisfies my logical correspondence principle. In this way, recalcitrant issues concerning the probabilities of conditionals are simply resolved. In particular, I have argued that for the Stalnaker language, LVCS, the probability of a conditional is the same as the corresponding conditional probability, provided that its probability is independent of the probability of its antecedent—which is surely the normal case.

On the classical approach, we require first a truth theory for a language in which our probability claims can be expressed. But while several notable attempts, including Carnap's, have been made to define such a language and provide such a truth theory, it is not clear that any of these attempts has been successful. The problem of specifying adequate truth conditions for probability claims has not yet been definitively resolved. Indeed, many philosophers interested in the problem have abandoned the attempt to solve it, and gone over to a subjectivist theory of probability, according to which a probability claim normally expresses a degree of belief. And, on this account, the rationality of a system of probability claims does not depend on whether these probability claims could all be true, but on whether the system of probability evaluations is coherent in a certain way. Hence, they have abandoned the attempt to construct a *unified* theory of the rationality of a belief system, and accepted that what makes a system of truth and falsity evaluations rational is quite different from what makes a system of probability evaluations so. The theory of rational belief systems is a unifying theory in the sense that if provides the same kind of criteria for the rationality of a system of truth and falsity evaluations as it does for a system of probability evaluations.

It may be objected that my theory of rational belief systems commits me to a subjectivist theory of truth since its extension to probability claims yields a subjectivist foundation for probability theory. But since, as I have argued, the theory is independent of any theory of truth, this is not so, and I can afford to remain agnostic whether there is an objective property of truth which is possessed or lacked by the sentences (or the beliefs expressed by them) of a given language. I would argue, likewise, that acceptance of a subjectivist foundation for probability theory does not commit anyone to the belief that probability claims have no objective truth or falsity. One who accepts such a foundation simply makes no commitment on this issue.

The theory of rational belief systems has been developed as part of a larger programme to write a scientific epistemology, i.e., a scientific theory about the structure and dynamics of human belief systems. Such an epistemology involves the total rejection of *a priorism*, even in the field of logic, and a rejection of the dualistic conception of man as an agent freely constructing his view of reality from data given to him through sense experience. In this essay, I have talked mainly about the structure of human belief systems, and proposed the theory that the laws of logic are the laws governing their structure. But I have said relatively little about the dynamics of our belief systems, about how they change or evolve. What I have had to say has been mainly negative.

It seems fairly clear that inductive reasoning never occurs in a pure form in an ideally rational being. If we appear to be drawing inferences, or making probability estimates, according to some inductive rule, it is only because we have some theoretical reasons for thinking that the sample we have taken most probably bears the required relationship to the population from which it has been drawn. Inductive projection always requires theoretical backing. In the absence of theoretical backing, any projection is as good as any other. This is the lesson to be learned from the Goodman paradoxes. Consequently, a rational man will strive to retain some theoretical understanding of the world, and project in accordance with it. Therefore, his anticipations of nature, of what will happen or will be found to have happened, will be as much in accord with his theoretical understanding of the world as what he already believes to have happened. He will, in this sense, operate theoretically conservatively. Thus, he will not reject any theory which he considers to have proven worth until he has something better to put in its place.

This is not to say that he will not strive to improve his theories, to make them more in accord with what he believes to have happened. On the contrary, if, to anticipate nature, he wishes to narrow as much as possible, without eliminating the range of theoretically compatible projections he can make, he will strive to develop a theoretical understanding of the world which is as precise in the predictions it yields, and as comprehensive in its application as possible.

These conclusions concerning the principles of inductive projection, which determine the dynamics of rational belief systems, are ill-defined, tentative and programmatic. But in broad outline they are probably correct. More precise formulations of these principles will have to await more thorough historical and psychological investigations of human thought processes. The required principles of inductive projection are just those idealized processes of thought which best explain ordinary human thinking.

NOTE

1. Duhem (1914), pp. 70–1.

BIBLIOGRAPHY

Adams, E.W. (1964) "On the Reasonableness of Inferences Involving Conditionals", *Proceedings of the 13th International Congress of Philosophy.*

—— (1965) "The Logic of Conditionals", *Inquiry*, vol. 8, pp. 166–97.

—— (1966) "Probability and the Logic of Conditionals" in J. Hintikka and P. Suppes (eds.), *Aspects of Inductive Logic* (Amsterdam, North Holland), pp. 265–316.

—— (1970) "Subjunctive and Indicative Conditionals", *Foundations of Language*, vol. 6, pp. 89–94

—— (1975) *The Logic of Conditionals: An Application of Probability to Deductive Logic* (Dordrecht, Holland; Boston; D. Reidel Pub. Co.).

Alston, William P. (1976) "Two Types of Foundationalism", *Journal of Philosophy*, vol. 73, pp. 165–85.

Aune, Bruce (1967) *Knowledge, Mind and Nature* (New York: Random House).

Ayers, M.R. (1965) "Counterfactuals and Subjunctive Conditionals", *Mind*, vol. 74, pp. 347–64.

Bohnen, Alfred (1969) "On the Critique of Modern Empiricism", *Ratio*, vol. 11, pp. 38–57.

Brandom, Robert (1976) "Truth and Assertability", *Journal of Philosophy*, vol. 73, pp. 137–49.

Carnap, Rudolf (1936-7) "Testability and Meaning", *Philosophy of Science*, vol. 3 and vol. 4. Reprinted with omissions in Feigl, H. and Brodbeck, M. (eds.), *Readings in the Philosophy of Science* (New York: Appleton-Century-Crofts, 1953), pp. 47–92.

Carnap, Rudolf (1950) *The Logical Foundations of Probability* (Chicago: University Press).

—— (1952) *The Continuum of Inductive Methods* (Chicago: University Press).

Chisholm, R.M. (1966) *Theory of Knowledge* (Englewood Cliffs, N.J., Prentice-Hall)

Creary, L.G. *and* C.S. Hill (1975) "Review of D.K. Lewis' *Counterfactuals*", *Philosophy of Science*, vol. 42, pp. 341–4.

Davidson, Donald (1965) "Theories of Meaning and Learnable

Languages" in *Logic, Methodology and Philosophy of Science*, edited by Y. Bar-Hillel (Amsterdam), pp. 383–94.

—— (1967) "Truth and Meaning", *Synthese*, vol. 17, pp. 304–23. Reprinted in *Philosophical Logic*, edited by J.W. Davis, D.J. Hocking and W.K. Wilson (Dordrecht, Holland: D. Reidel, 1969), pp. 1–20. References are to the Davis, Hocking and Wilson volume.

—— (1969a) "On Saying That", in *Words and Objections*, edited by D. Davidson and J. Hintikka (Dordrecht, Holland: Reidel), pp. 158–74.

—— (1969b) "True to the Facts", *Journal of Philosophy*, vol. 66, pp. 748–64.

—— (1973) "In Defence of Convention T" in *Truth, Syntax and Modality*, edited by H. Leblanc (Amsterdam; North Holland), pp. 76–85.

Duhem, P. (1914) *The Aim and Structure of Physical Theory* (Princeton, New Jersey; Princeton University Press, 1954), trans. P.P. Wiener from the second edition of *La Théorie Physique: Son Objet, Sa Structure* (Paris, 1914).

Ellis, B.D. (1963) "Universal and Differential Forces", *British Journal for the Philosophy of Science*, vol. 14, pp. 177–94.

—— (1965a) "The Origin and Nature of Newton's Laws of Motion", in R.G. Colodny (ed.), *Beyond the Edge of Certainty*, (Englewood Cliffs, N.J.; Prentice-Hall), pp. 29–68.

—— (1965b) "A Vindication of Scientific Inductive Practices", *American Philosophical Quarterly*, vol. 2, pp.1–9.

—— (1966) *Basic Concepts of Measurement* (Cambridge; The University Press).

—— (1969) "An Epistemological Concept of Truth" in Robert Brown and C.D. Rollins (eds.), *Contemporary Philosophy in Australia* (London; Allen and Unwin), pp. 52–72.

—— (1973) "The Logic of Subjective Probability", *British Journal for the Philosophy of Science*, vol. 24, pp. 125–52.

—— (1975) "Physicalism and the Contents of Sense Experience", in *Philosophical Aspects of the Mind-Body Problem*, edited by Chung-ying Cheng (Honolulu; The University Press of Hawaii), pp. 64–77.

—— (1976a) "Epistemic Foundations of Logic", *Journal of Philosophical Logic*, vol. 5, pp. 187–204.

—— (1976b) "The Existence of Forces", *Studies in the History and Philosophy of Science*, vol. 7, pp. 171–85.

Ellis, B.D. and B. Davidson (1976) "Logic and Strict Coherence", *Reports on Mathematical Logic*, vol. 6, pp. 29–40.

Ellis, B.D., F.C. Jackson and R. Pargetter (1977) "An Objection to Possible-Worlds Semantics for Counterfactual Logics", *Journal of Philosophical Logic*, vol. 6.

Einstein, A. (1905) "On the Electrodynamics of Moving Bodies", translated by W. Perrett and G.B. Jeffery from the original in *Annalen der Physik*, vol. 17 (first published by Methuen and Co., 1923; republished by Dover).

Feyerabend, P.K. (1962) "Explanation, Reduction and Empiricism", in H. Feigl and G. Maxwell (eds.), *Minnesota Studies in the Philosophy of Science*, vol. 3, pp. 28–97.

—— (1965) "Problems of Empiricism", in *Beyond the Edge of Certainty*, edited by R.G. Colodny (New Jersey: Prentice Hall), pp. 145–260.

Fine, K. (1975) Critical Notice of Lewis, D., *Counterfactuals*, *Mind*, vol. 84, pp. 451–8.

de Finetti, Bruno (1937) "Foresight: Its Logical Laws, Its Subjective Sources", in H.E. Kyburg and H. Smokler (eds.) *Studies in Subjective Probability* (New York; John Wiley and Sons, 1964), pp. 93–158.

Frege, G. (1884) *The Foundations of Arithmetic* (Oxford, 1950) translated by J.L. Austin from the German *Die Grundlagen der Arithmetik* (Breslau, 1884).

Goodman, N. (1947) "The Problem of Counterfactual Conditionals", *Journal of Philosophy*, vol. 44, pp. 113–28.

—— (1955) *Fact, Fiction and Forecast* (Cambridge, Mass.: Harvard University Press).

Hacking, I. (1968) "One Problem About Induction", *The Problem of Inductive Logic*, edited by Imre Lakatos (Amsterdam; North Holland), pp. 44–59.

Hume. D. (1777) *Enquiry Concerning Human Understanding*, (Oxford; The Clarendon Press, 1975). Reprinted from the 1777 edition with Introduction and Analytic Index by L.A. Selby-Bigge.

Husserl, E. (1900–1) *Logische Untersuchungen*, 2 vols. (Halle).

Jackson, F.C. (1977) "A Causal Theory of Counterfactuals", *Australasian Journal of Philosophy*, vol. 55, pp. 3–21.

Kuhn, T.S. (1962) *The Structure of Scientific Revolutions* (Chicago: University of Chicago Press).

Lakatos, I. (1970) "Falsification and the Methodology of Scientific Research Programmes" in I. Lakatos and A. Musgrave (eds.),

Criticism and the Growth of Knowledge (Cambridge; The University Press), pp. 91–196.

Lakatos, I. *and* A. Musgrave (eds.) (1970) *Criticism and the Growth of Knowledge* (Cambridge; The University Press).

Lewis, D.K. (1971) "Immodest Inductive Methods", *Philosophy of Science*, vol. 38, pp. 54–63.

—— (1973) *Counterfactuals* (Cambridge, Mass.; Harvard University Press).

—— (1974) "Spielman and Lewis on Inductive Immodesty", *Philosophy of Science*, vol. 41, pp. 84–5.

—— (1976a) "Counterfactual Dependence and Time's Arrow". Paper read to Australasian Association for the History and Philosophy of Science Conference in Melbourne, August, 1976.

—— (1976b) "Probabilities of Conditionals and Conditional Probabilities", *Philosophical Review*, vol. 85, pp. 297–315.

Lipps, Theodore (1880) "Die Aufgabe der Erkenntnistheorie", *Philosophische Monatshefte*, vol. 16.

Loewer, B. (1976) "Counterfactuals with Disjunctive Antecedents", *Journal of Philosophy*, vol. 73, pp. 531–7.

McKay, T. *and* P. Van Inwagen (1977) "Counterfactuals with Disjunctive Antecedents", *Philosophical Studies*, vol. 31, pp. 353–6.

McKinsey, J.C.C., A.C. Sugar *and* P. Suppes (1953) "Axiomatic Foundations of Classical Mechanics", *Journal of Rational Mechanics and Analysis*, vol. 2, pp. 253–72.

Mill, J.S. (1843) *A System of Logic* (London).

—— (1865) *Examination of Sir William Hamilton's Philosophy* (London).

Nute, D. (1975) "Counterfactuals and the Similarity of Worlds", *Journal of Philosophy*, vol. 72, pp. 773–8.

Pastin, M. (1974) "Foundationalism Redux", *Journal of Philosophy*, vol. 71, pp. 709–10.

Pollock, J.L. (1976) *Subjunctive Reasoning* (Dordrecht, Holland; D. Reidel Publishing Company).

Popper, K.R. (1934) *The Logic of Scientific Discovery* (London; Hutchinson, 1959) translated by the author from *Logik der Forschung* (Vienna, 1934).

—— (1955) "Two Autonomous Axiom Systems for Probability", *British Journal for the Philosophy of Science*, vol. 6, pp. 51–7.

—— (1963a) *Conjectures and Refutations* (London; Routledge and Kegan Paul).

—— (1963b) "Creative and Non-Creative Definitions in the Calculus of Probability", *Synthese,* vol. 15, pp. 167–86.

Quine, W.V.O. (1953) "Two Dogmas of Empiricism", in *From a Logical Point of View* (Cambridge, Mass.; Harvard University Press), pp.20–46.

—— (1954) "The Scope and Language of Science", in *Ways of Paradox and Other Essays* (New York; Random House, 1966), pp. 215–32.

—— (1969) "Propositional Objects", in *Ontological Relativity and Other Essays* (New York and London; Columbia University Press), pp. 139–60.

Reichenbach, H. (1928) *The Philosophy of Space and Time* (New York; Dover, 1958), translated by Maria Reichenbach and John Freund from *Philosophie der Raum-Zeit-Lehre.*

—— (1935) *Theory of Probability* (Berkeley, University of California Press, 1949, 1971), translated by E.H. Hutten and M. Reichenbach from *Wahrscheinlichkeitslehre.*

—— (1938) *Experience and Prediction* (Chicago; University Press).

Rescher, N. (1964) *Hypothetical Reasoning* (Amsterdam; North Holland).

—— (1973) *The Coherence Theory of Truth* (Oxford; The Clarendon Press).

—— (1974) "Foundationalism, Coherentism, and the Idea of Cognitive Systematization", *Journal of Philosophy,* vol. 71, pp. 695–708.

Richards, T.J. (1969) "The Harmlessness of Material Implication", *Mind,* vol. 78, pp. 417–22.

Salmon, W.C. (1955) "The Short Run", *Philosophy of Science,* vol. 22.

—— (1961) "Vindication of Induction", *Current Issues in the Philosophy of Science* edited by H. Feigl and G. Maxwell (New York; Holt, Reinhart and Winsten), pp. 245–56.

—— (1963) "On Vindicating Induction", *Induction; Some Current Issues* edited by H. Kyburg and E. Nagel (Middletown; Wesleyan University Press).

Salmon, W.C. (1968) "The Justification of Inductive Rules of Inference", *The Problem of Inductive Logic* edited by Imre Lakatos (Amsterdam; North Holland), pp. 24–43.

Savage, L.J. (1961) "The Foundations of Statistics Reconsidered", in *Studies in Subjective Probability,* edited by H.E. Kyburg Jr.

and H.E. Smokler (New York; John Wiley and Sons, 1964), pp. 173–88.

Smart, J.J.C. (1963) *Philosophy and Scientific Realism* (London; Routledge and Kegan Paul).

—— (1968) *Between Science and Philosophy* (New York; Random House)

Spielman, S. (1972) "Lewis on Immodest Inductive Methods", *Philosophy of Science,* vol. 39, pp. 375–7.

Stalnaker, R.C. (1968) "A Theory of Conditionals", *Studies in Logical Theory,* American Philosophical Quarterly Monograph series, vol. 2 (Oxford; Blackwells), pp. 98–112.

—— (1970) "Probability and Conditionals", *Philosophy of Science,* vol. 37, pp. 64–80.

Stalnaker, R.C. *and* R.H. Thomason (1970) "A Semantic Analysis of Conditional Logic", *Theoria,* vol. 36, pp. 23–42.

Van Fraassen, B.C. (1974) "Hidden Variables in Conditional Logic", *Theoria,* vol. 40, pp. 176–90.

—— (1970) "Representation of Conditional Probabilities", *Journal of Philosophical Logic,* vol. 5, pp. 417–30.

NAME INDEX

SUBJECT INDEX